BECOME THE PERSON YOU WERE MEANT TO BE

BECOME THE PERSON YOU WERE MEANT TO BE

ESSENTIAL LIFE LESSONS YOU DIDN'T LEARN FROM YOUR PARENTS AND TEACHERS

DR. MYREN D. ANDERSON

Copyright © 2023

ALL RIGHTS RESERVED. No part of this story may be reproduced or transmitted in any form whatsoever, electronic or mechanical, including photocopying, recording, or any information storage or retrieval system without express written, dated, and signed permission from the author.

DISCLAIMER AND/OR LEGAL NOTICES: The information presented in this report represents the author's views as of the date of publication. The author/publisher reserves the right to alter and update their opinions based on new conditions. The author and the publisher do not accept any responsibility for any liabilities resulting from the use of this information. While every attempt has been made to verify the information provided here, the author and the publisher cannot assume any responsibility for errors, inaccuracies, or omissions. All relevant names, businesses, and most geographic locations have been changed for security and privacy reasons.

"This activity is made possible in part by a grant provided by the Northwest Minnesota Arts Council through funding from The McKnight Foundation."

www.juliamariedesign.com

This book is dedicated to the memory of my father, Elmer, who taught me the value of honest work and instilled in me a sense of moral strength and self-discipline. My mother, Frances was an example of someone who truly expressed unconditional love. She also stressed the importance of family and gave me the courage to attempt new things and inspired me to become a lifelong learner and a better person.

It is also dedicated to all who wish to improve their lives.

-Dr. Myren D. Anderson

INTRODUCTION

This is a book about personal growth. Its purpose is to help the reader develop good habits, attitudes, beliefs and skills to enhance their quality of life, to have greater overall success, and ultimately, to help them to become more of the person they are capable of becoming.

Thirty-four life-changing principles are explored with common sense advice from the author and numerous quotes of wisdom by various sages from the Buddha to Voltaire, as well as quotes from recent thinkers such as H. Jackson Brown Jr. to Andrew Weil, M.D.

Become the person you were meant to be!

-Dr. Myren D. Anderson

TABLE OF CONTENTS

1. YOU CAN'T FLY WITH EAGLES IF YOU HANG AROUND WITH TURKEYS
2. CHARACTER COUNTS
3. LEARN TO TALK YOURSELF UP SO OTHERS CAN'T TALK YOU DOWN
4. CHANGE YOUR THOUGHTS, CHANGE YOUR LIFE
5. IF IT IS TO BE, IT IS UP TO ME
6. TO GROW: ACT ONE STEP BIGGER THAN YOU FEEL; PUSH YOURSELF BEYOND YOUR COMFORT ZONE
7. WHAT YOU "SEE" IS WHAT YOU GET
8. OUR PURPOSE DETERMINES OUR GOALS AND OUR DESTINY
9. SCHOOL IS NEVER OUT FOR THE PRO
10. DAILY DOSES OF MOTIVATION AND INSPIRATION ARE NEEDED
11. THE JOY OF WORK
12. WINNERS NEVER QUIT; QUITTERS NEVER WIN
13. THERE ARE NO FAILURES OR MISTAKES, ONLY LESSONS
14. RISK TAKING IS ESSENTIAL FOR SUCCESS
15. NEVER MAKE A NEGATIVE DECISION IN A "DOWN" TIME
16. TRUST YOUR INTUITION
17. YESTERDAY'S ANSWER MAY NOT WORK TODAY
18. LEARN TO OVERCOME ADVERSITY
19. KNOW WHEN TO HOLD ON AND WHEN TO LET GO
20. PRESENT TIME CONSCIOUSNESS (PTC)
21. ANTICIPATE THE GOOD EVEN DURING THE BAD
22. THE POWER OF SIMPLICITY
23. COMPLETE CYCLES
24. THREE DEADLY EMOTIONS: FEAR, WORRY AND GUILT
25. SUCCESS: LIVING YOUR LIFE AS YOU SEE FIT
26. COUNT YOUR BLESSINGS
27. YOU ARE NEVER WEALTHY UNLESS YOU ARE HEALTHY
28. YOU CAN'T LOVE ANOTHER UNTIL YOU LEARN TO LOVE YOURSELF
29. HAPPINESS IS A JOURNEY…NOT A DESTINATION
30. NO SUCCESS IN LIFE CAN COMPENSATE FOR FAILURE IN THE HOME
31. A GREAT LIFE REQUIRES A LOT OF FORGIVENESS
32. ENJOYING LIFE IS A SKILL…THE ART OF LIVING WELL
33. YOU NEED A FAITH TO LIVE BY
34. GROWING OLD GRACEFULLY

"He that lies down with dogs shall rise up with fleas." –Anonymous

"It is better to weep with wise men than to laugh with fools."–Spanish Proverb

1

YOU CAN'T FLY WITH EAGLES IF YOU HANG AROUND WITH TURKEYS

Many a father and a mother have lamented the fact that their son or daughter had gotten into the wrong crowd. Everyone needs to feel a part of a group and sometimes peer pressure is stronger than common sense. It is vitally important we have enough self-esteem, so we associate with people who are basically good.

W. Clement Stone reminded us, "Be careful the environment you choose for it will shape you; be careful the friends you choose for you will become like them." George Washington offers us this wisdom, "Associate yourself with men of good qualities if you esteem your own reputation, or, 'tis better to be alone than in bad company."

Make sure you don't act like a sheep and follow the flock over the cliff. One foolish act can ruin a person's life. Never sacrifice your reputation and self-image for the sake of a short-term gain or pleasure. The decisions you make ultimately determine the life you will have. It is you and you alone who will determine your destiny.

You can't hang out with negative people and expect to have a positive life. It is always your choice as to who you spend time with and it's always best to surround yourself with people who bring out the best in you. Keep people in your life who encourage you and make you feel good about yourself, otherwise let them go.

Plato said, "People are like dirt. They can either nourish you and help you grow as a person, or they can stunt your growth and make you wilt and die." Find a mentor, someone you can look up to and admire and then act and behave in a similar manner. Wayne Dyer put it like this: "When you allow toxic people into your immediate energy field you will find that your feelings of well-being diminish." Life is too short to spend time with people who suck the life out of you with their negativity and gloom. On the other hand, if you hang around with positive and successful people you will feel like doing something yourself. So never underestimate the power of influence of another individual. You have a choice who you will spend time with so choose wisely and you will be better for it. It is extremely important one stays away from pessimistic and other toxic people who always find something wrong with the world and feel like everything and everyone is against them. It's much better to hang around with positive people who tend to charge your batteries. Negative people tend to 'rain on our parade' and discourage us and weaken our resolve to succeed.

Confide in people who are happy for your success and ambitions as they will give you support and encouragement. Remember the words of Buddha, "Shun worthless associates with their empty talk and mundane ambitions."

Imagine having lunch with a friend one day and you mention the fact you are thinking of building a new home. Suppose this "friend" reminded you how much planning was involved, how hard it is to find good carpenters, the high interest rates, increased taxes and so on. Do you think you would still be interested in building? Some people are so negative that if they were reincarnated, they would come back as a wet blanket.

On the other hand, suppose your friend encouraged you, commenting on the extra space you'd have, the ease of maintenance of newer homes, and the joy of owning a new home? Now how would you feel? Be sure to discuss your great dreams with positive thinkers only. They will encourage you rather than try to shoot down your plans. As Mark Twain said, "Keep away from people who try to belittle your ambitions. Small people always do that, but the really great make you feel that you, too, can become great."

Perhaps, you've made some mistakes in your life but now you recognize the errors of your past and you'd like to change. Realizing and acknowledging your mistakes are the first steps to a new beginning. Now it's time to move on and to pick yourself up by the bootstraps and get to work. Mistakes help us to grow as they are part of life's lessons. We are all human and we have within us the seeds of our own growth and the virus of our own destruction. It depends on which we are going to emphasize. Keep on keeping on as there is great hope for you. As Plutarch said, "The wildest colts make the best horses."

It's good to remember that you are an original and have a special purpose to fulfill on planet Earth. No one will ever be like you; God does not make carbon copies so don't try to copy others. It is because we are all different that makes each of us so special. Be who you are and all you can be! Dr. Seuss put it best: "Why fit in when you were born to stand out." And who can forget these famous lines by Dr. Seuss: "You have brains in your head. You have feet in your shoes. You can steer yourself in any direction you choose. You're on your own, and you know what you know. And you are the guy who will decide where to go."

"Other people's views and troubles can be contagious. Don't sabotage yourself by unwittingly adopting negative, unproductive attitudes through your associations with others." - Epictetus

"Without doubt, the most common weakness of all human beings is the habit of leaving their minds open to the negative influence of other people." - Napoleon Hill

"Your outlook upon life, your estimate of yourself, your estimate of your value are largely colored by your environment. Your whole career will be modified, shaped, molded by your surroundings, by the character of the people with whom you come in contact every day." - Orison Swett Marden

"Align yourself with people that you can learn from, people who want more out of life, people who are stretching and searching and seeking some higher ground in life." - Les Brown

TAKEAWAY: SURROUND YOURSELF WITH POSITIVE INDIVIDUALS.

Dr. Myren D. Anderson

"Character is the ability to carry out a good resolution long after the excitement of the moment has passed." – Cavett Robert

"Be more concerned with your character than your reputation, because your character is what you really are, while your reputation is nearly what others think you are." – John Wooden

2

CHARACTER COUNTS

Character refers to the moral and ethical quality of a person, including honesty and integrity. A man or woman of character does what he or she says they will do. They can be trusted. This is a very important quality.

As Buddha said, "Sound health is the greatest of gifts; contentedness, the greatest of riches; trust, the greatest of qualities." If you are a person of integrity, you'll never have to go back and cover your tracks. If you maintain integrity in your business deals, you'll never do wrong. A sage once said, "We should live a good and honorable life, then when you get older and think back, you will enjoy it a second time."

Leonardo Da Vinci said, "As a well spent day brings happy sleep, so a life well spent brings happy death." We tend to grow during times of adversity, and this develops our character. Poverty and wealth are also great tests of character and tend to bring out the best or worst in us. It's helpful to create a 'to do' list every day. Check off whatever it was you were going to do that day as this is a good discipline which helps you to do what you say you are going to do. Lao-tzu offers us this wisdom: "He who conquers others is strong; he who conquers himself is mighty."

"Let us endeavor so to live that when we come to die even the undertaker will be sorry." - Mark Twain

Character building is a lifelong do-it-yourself project. We must continually work on self-improvement from childhood to our last day. Self-discipline is a big part of our character. We have to walk the walk and do what we say we are going to do.

Napoleon Hill said, "Attend well to your character and your reputation will look out for itself." Abraham Lincoln put it this way: "Character is like a tree and reputation like a shadow. The shadow is what we think of it; the tree is the real thing." When you think of individuals of great character, people like Thomas Jefferson, George Washington, Abraham Lincoln, Benjamin Franklin, Harry Truman and Rev. Billy Graham comes to mind. They are looked up by many because of their honesty, integrity and their moral values.

"When wealth is lost, nothing is lost; when health is lost, something is lost; when character is lost, all is lost." - Rev. Billy Graham

Here are two favorite poems of mine which illustrate character.

The Man in The Glass
By: Peter Dale Wimbrow Sr.

When you get what you want in your struggle for self
And the world makes you king for a day,
Just go to a mirror and look at yourself
And see what that man has to say...
For it isn't your father, or mother, or wife
Whose judgment upon you must pass,
The fellow whose verdict counts most in your life
Is the one staring back from the glass.
He's the fellow to please-never mind all the rest
For he's with you, clear to the end
And you've passed your most difficult, dangerous test.
If the man in the glass is your friend...
You may fool the whole world down
the pathway of years
And get pats on the back as you pass
But your final reward will be heartache and tears
If you've cheated the man in the glass.

The Measure of Man
Not "How did he die?" But "How did he live?"
Not "What did he gain?" But "What did he give?"
Not "What was his station?" But "Had he a heart?"
And "How did he play his God-given part?"
Not "What was his shrine?" More "What was his creed?"
But "Had he befriended those really in need?"
Not "What did the sketch in the newspaper say?"
But "How many were sorry, when he passed away?"
Was he ever ready with a word or good cheer, to bring back a smile, to vanish a tear?
These are the units to measure the worth of a man as a man regardless of birth. - Anonymous

I'd like to end this chapter with a favorite story of mine.

The Carpenter

An elderly carpenter was ready to retire. He told his employer-contractor of his plans to leave the house-building business and live a more leisurely life with his wife enjoying his extended family. He would miss the paycheck, but he needed to retire. They could get by.

The contractor was sorry to see his good worker go and asked if he would build just one more house as a personal favor. The carpenter said yes, but in time it was easy to see that his heart was not in his work. He resorted to shoddy workmanship and used inferior materials. It was an unfortunate way to end his career.

When the carpenter finished his work and the builder came to inspect the house the contractor handed the front-door key to the carpenter, "This is your house," he said. "My gift to you".

What a shock! What a shame! If he had only known he was building his own house, he would have done it all so differently. Now he had to live in the home that he had built none too well.

So, it is with us. We build our lives in a distracted way, reacting rather than acting, willing to put forth less than our best. At important points we do not give the job our best effort. Then with a shock, we look at the situation we have created and find we are now living in the house we have built. If we had realized that we would have done it differently.

Think of yourself as the carpenter. Think about your house. Each day you hammer a nail, place a board, erect a wall. Build it wisely. It is the only life you will ever build. Even if you live it for only one more day, that day deserves to be lived graciously and with dignity.

The plaque on the wall says, "Life is a do-it-yourself project."

Who could say it more clearly? Your life today is a result of your attitudes and choices in the past. Your life tomorrow will be the result of your attitudes and the choices you make today. - Author Unknown

TAKEAWAY: A MAN WITHOUT CHARACTER CHEATS HIMSELF IN THE END.

Dr. Myren D. Anderson

"By your words you will be justified, and by your words you will be condemned." –(MT 12:37)

"Death and Life are in the power of the tongue."
–Solomon

3

LEARN TO TALK YOURSELF UP SO OTHERS CAN'T TALK YOU DOWN

You talk to yourself all the time. You are either talking yourself up or you are talking yourself down. If you change the words you use when you talk to yourself, your experience will change. What you tell yourself will determine how far you will go and how long it will take to get you there. The words one speaks to oneself make a deep impression on your mind. Your words can actually change your world. You are condemned by negative words.

What we feed our mind is just as important as what we feed our bodies. It is your responsibility to nurture yourself as it empowers you. Monitor how you talk to yourself. Listen to what you say to yourself. Look in the mirror and give yourself a pep talk. Say something positive to yourself," I am full of power today" or "It's like me to always be on time." If you change the way you talk, your experience will change.

Negative people tend to talk us down to make themselves look better. Listening to the doubts of others can destroy our dreams. Never tell a negative person about any of your plans or dreams as they will happily point out several reasons why your ideas aren't any good and won't work out. This instills doubt in your mind and kills the dream. Shakespeare offers this wisdom, "Our doubts are traitors, and make us lose the good we oft might win by fearing to attempt."

A good way to talk yourself up is to use affirmations. An affirmation is a positive declaration you make to yourself. It means to validate or to confirm. The purpose of an affirmation is to reprogram your mind by replacing negative beliefs with positive beliefs.

Affirmations build you up and fortify you if used repeatedly. Whatever you impress on your subconscious mind will be expressed. Repeating affirmations daily is a good way of talking positively to oneself. Affirmations can restore our confidence and help to eliminate our fears and worries. Affirmations can counteract negativity from well-meaning friends and associates. You can create your own affirmations. The following are very good.

> "Every day in every way, I'm getting healthier and healthier."
> "I feel good. I feel great. I feel terrific."
> "My food is naturally salty."
> "I monitor my words and keep them positive."
> "I have pep in my step and a smile all the while."
> "I am under the influence of divine wisdom."

How you talk to yourself will determine your experience in life and if you don't program your mind positively, others will program it negatively. Louise Hay said, "We create our experiences by our thoughts." Use affirmations daily; you'll be happier, more successful, and healthier.

> "I am only one, but I am one.
> I can't do everything, but I can do something.
> What I can do, I ought to do.
> And what I ought to do,
> by the grace of God I will do."
> -Canor Farrer

> "Evidence is conclusive that your self-talk
> has a direct bearing on your performance."
> -Zig Ziglar

TAKEAWAY: WHAT YOU TELL YOURSELF WILL DETERMINE HOW FAR YOU WILL GO.

Dr. Myren D. Anderson

"The key to every man is his thought." –Emerson

"We are what we think. All that we are arises with our thoughts. With our thoughts, we make the world." –Buddha

4

CHANGE YOUR THOUGHTS, CHANGE YOUR LIFE

A sage once said, "Most of our troubles are caused by our thinking."

Basically, there are two general ways a person can think — positive thinking or negative thinking. Positive thinking helps us to improve our lives whereas negative never results in improvement. Success depends on the quality of our thoughts as our thoughts determine our experience. Your life reflects what goes on in your head as how we look at things is determined by our state of mind.

Here's a quote which illustrates this well: "Two men looked out from prison bars; one saw the mud, the other saw stars." Our state of mind is determined by our attitude and how we think. William James said, "The greatest discovery of my generation is that a human being can alter his life by altering his attitude of mind." What we think will determine what we do. Quality thoughts produce quality results.

Plutarch wrote, "What we achieve inwardly will change outer reality." What you think about comes about as our lives are controlled by our current predominant thoughts. Ernest Holmes said, "Life is a mirror and will reflect back to the thinker what he thinks into it." Keep your thoughts positive, optimistic, constructive and kind.

Change the quality of your thoughts and you will change your life's direction and your destiny. What you think determines what you do and how you do it. If you think in terms of optimistic thoughts, it is more likely you will live a happy and productive life. Negative thoughts, on the other hand, produce unhappiness and ultimate failure. Focusing on the negative gets you more negative. We need to replace negative thoughts with positive ones, as we cannot entertain a negative thought without getting a negative result. Peace Pilgrim said, "If you realized how powerful your thoughts are, you would never think a negative thought." What we sow in mind we will reap in manifestation. Always feel like you are riding the crest of the wave.

Depending on how we view the world in our thoughts, we are either an optimist or a pessimist. In general, optimists are positive, and pessimists are negative. Winston Churchill observed, "A pessimist sees the difficulty in every opportunity; an optimist sees the opportunity in every difficulty." Mark Twain said, "There is no sadder sight than a young pessimist." In order to become a more positive person we need to change our programming. Listening to inspiring audio tapes and watching self-help videos can help to program a person's life positively and aids in self-development. Self-help books are also helpful. Daily affirmations tend to help a person be more positive as well. It is also important that we watch the words we use on a habitual basis. Joel Osteen put it this way, "You can change your world by changing your words … Remember, death and life are in the power of the tongue." Always replace a negative thought with a positive one. Don't spend time thinking about what's wrong with the world.

Negative emotions like fear and guilt are two of the most destructive thoughts we can have. Fear (false evidence appearing real) is worry about the future and guilt is thinking about some offense you've done in the past, either illegal, unethical or immoral. The solution is to keep your mind on the present (present mind consciousness.) Many times fear thoughts tend to bring about what is feared. If you don't want it…don't think about it.

Eddie Rickenbacker, the famous World War I hero said, "I believe that if you think about disaster, you will get it. Brood about death and you will hasten your demise. Think positively and masterfully with confidence and faith, and life becomes more secure, more fraught with action, richer in achievement and experience."

As the old Chinese Proverb states, "Misfortunes come to all men." It's important for us to realize this and to avoid the negative thinking which tends to come when things don't turn out exactly like we'd like. As Epictetus said, "We are not troubled by things, but by the opinion which we have of things." When things turn out really bad, we have to have faith that things will eventually turn around. William Hazlitt reminds us, "If you think you can win, you can win. Faith is necessary for victory."

Never let the mass media mind influence your thoughts and behavior. Thinking about poverty, sickness, disaster, war, etc., tends to drag you down mentally. Watching the evening news with all its gloom and doom is a recipe for negativity. Your life will reflect what you think about as your mind magnifies what it looks upon. By changing our thoughts, we can change our behavior and ultimately our actions and outcomes.

> "If you are distressed by anything external, the pain is not due to the thing itself but to your own estimate of it; and this you have the power to revoke at any moment."
> -Marcus Aurelius

> "You are today where your thoughts have brought you; you will be tomorrow where your thoughts take you."
> -James Allen

> "Watch your thoughts, they become your words; watch your words, they become your actions; watch your actions, they become your habits; watch your habits, they become your character; watch your character, it becomes your destiny."
> -Lao Tzu

"Thinking: the talking of the soul with itself."
-Plato

By Changing Your Thinking,
you can change your beliefs;
When you change your beliefs,
you change your expectations;
When you change your expectations,
you change your attitude;
When you change your attitude,
you change your behavior;
When you change your behavior,
you change your performance;
When you change your performance,
You Change Your Life!

"Surely as I have thought, so shall it come to pass."
-Isaiah 14:24

TAKEAWAY: WHAT WE SOW IN MIND, WE WILL REAP IN MANIFESTATION.

Dr. Myren D. Anderson

"God gives every bird his food, but he does not throw it into the nest."-Josiah Gilbert Holland

"The fault, dear Brutus, is not in our stars, but in ourselves that we are underlings."
-William Shakespeare

5

IF IT IS TO BE, IT IS UP TO ME

In order for us to be, do and have we cannot depend on others; we must rely on our own talents and resources. God has given us all the gifts and abilities we need to lead a happy and successful life. The world is the same for all of us.

Louis L'Amour is credited with saying, "Up to a point, a man's life is shaped by environment, heredity and movement and changes in the world about him. Then there comes a time when it lies within his grasp to shape the clay of his life into the sort of thing he wishes to be…everyone has within his power to say, 'this I am today, that I shall be tomorrow.'" James Allen put it like this: "A man sooner or later discovers that he is the master gardener of his soul, the director of his life." So, if it is to be…it is up to me! There is an old Irish Proverb which says, "You've got to do your own growing, no matter how tall your grandfather was."

We need to get excited about who we are and what we do. You have to believe in yourself. You have to believe you have what it takes to design your own destiny. The amount of success and satisfaction you get from life depends on your vision, self-deficiency, resourcefulness, ambition and ingenuity. George Bernard Shaw observed: "The people who get on in this world are the people who get up and look for the circumstances they want, and, if they can't find them, make them." It is our duty to try and make our life a masterpiece. We need to spend time with successful people so we feel like doing something ourselves. We need to dream big dreams and if a dream dies, we need to dream another dream. Always ask for more than you expect to get. Just keep asking and the law of averages will get you enough "yes" answers to get you where you want to go. Dare to expect greater good coming to you. Let your imagination run wild. Know that whatever you focus on will come into your life. You get what you prepare for.

It is absolutely vital that a person becomes immune to discouragement. We cannot allow adverse appearances to cause us to falter as our own doubts and fears are our own worst enemies. Keep your eye on the doughnut, and not upon the hole, as they say. We need to hang on long after others would have let go. Feel that the tide of destiny has turned and that everything is coming your way. Keep your mind on something always going right. Know that if things are not going well, it's not him, her or the government; it's you! Always act as if it's impossible to fail. Reverend Robert H. Schuller said, "The biggest and best dreams are thrown away because we are not possibility thinkers." I like what Famous Amos had to say about self reliance. "It is important to believe in yourself. Believe that you can do it, under any circumstances. Because, if you believe you can, then you really will. That belief just keeps you searching for the answers and pretty soon you'll get it."

Nothing great or anything of value was ever achieved by anyone without the act of setting goals and acting upon them. Thomas Carlyle observed, "A man without goals is like a ship without a rudder." We need to set specific written goals with deadlines if we are to accomplish anything in this life. Both short- and long-term goals are needed. When we achieve a short-term goal it gives us energy to keep working on our long range goals. In order to achieve any goal we need to have a purpose in our life. A good purpose is to make a difference in other people's lives. It takes discipline to stay on purpose. You will know you are on purpose when work is fun and time passes quickly. If you are bored, stressed out and hate to go to work, you are off-purpose. Robert Byrne is credited with saying, "The purpose of life is a life of purpose."

If it is to be, we must continue to learn throughout life. School is never out for the pro. There is no such thing as saturation when it comes to learning. As Newton E. Baker said so well, "The man who graduates today and stops learning tomorrow is uneducated the day after." It is important to read books, listen to tapes and to attend seminars. The purpose of learning is personal growth. Life should be a continuous learning experience from the basket to the casket.

Education is a journey — not a destination. It is vital we keep an open mind. Sidney J. Harris said it well when he reminded us that, "The most valuable form of education is the kind that puts the educator inside you, as it were, so that the appetite for learning persists long after the external pressure for grades and degrees has vanished. Otherwise you are not educated, you are merely trained." Our learning must lead to action. Someone once said, "Do not ask the Lord to guide your footsteps if you are not willing to move your feet." The following Chinese rhyme by an anonymous author says it pretty well also:

> "This one makes a net,
> this one stands and wishes.
> Would you like to bet
> which one gets the fishes."

It is imperative we work to make ourselves better as the years go by. As we age, we either make ourselves better or we become bitter. Each of us has the seeds of good or bad (saint or sinner) within. We need to minimize negative traits such as hate, greed, anger, apathy, fear, guilt, worry, etc., and work to develop the positive traits such as love, humility, peace, compassion, trust, kindness, generosity and gratitude. I came across the following little story which tells it best:

The Wolf You Feed

The Wolves Inside You

An elder Native American was teaching his grandchildren about life. He said to them, "A fight is going on inside me ... it is a terrible fight and it is between two wolves. One wolf represents fear, anger, envy, sorrow, regret, greed, arrogance, self-pity, guilt, resentment, inferiority, lies, false pride, superiority and ego.

The other stands for joy, peace, love, hope, sharing, serenity, humility, kindness, benevolence, friendship, empathy, generosity, truth, compassion and faith."

"'This same fight is going on inside you, and inside every other person, too'", he added.

The grandchildren thought about it for a minute and then one child asked his grandfather, "Which wolf will win?"

The old Cherokee simply replied ... "'The one you feed.'"

-Anonymous

"A #2 pencil and a dream can take you anywhere."
-Joyce Meyer

"I'd rather attempt to do something great and fail than to attempt to do nothing and succeed."
-Robert H. Schuller

"The ladder of success cannot be climbed with your hands in your pocket."
-Unknown Author

TAKEAWAY: LIFE IS A DO IT YOURSELF PROJECT.

Dr. Myren D. Anderson

"If you always do what you've always done, you'll always get what you always got."
-Ed Foreman

"Nature will give you what you act like you already have." -Dr. James W. Parker

6

TO GROW: ACT ONE STEP BIGGER THAN YOU FEEL; PUSH YOURSELF BEYOND YOUR COMFORT ZONE

To grow and to become better, we must act like we already are. If we act confidently, we will become more confident. If we act successful, we will become more successful. We must first "be" before we can "do" and we must "do" before we can "have." This is called the be – do and have principle. To achieve greatly, we must act one step bigger than we feel. The key word here is act as action cures fear and gets a person excited and on the way.

Robert J. McKain wrote, "The common conception is that motivation leads to action, but the reverse is true — action precedes motivation. You have to 'prime the pump' and get the juices flowing, which motivates you to work on your goals. Getting momentum going is the most difficult part of the job, and often taking the first step is enough to prompt you to make the most of your day."

To reach our full potential, we must push ourselves beyond our comfort zone. In our efforts to become a more valuable employee or a more effective leader, we must render more service than is customary. We must go the "extra mile." If you do this, you will really stand out in the crowd as most people only do just enough to get by. When you go the extra mile, you have given yourself a successful experience. This adds to your confidence and enhances your self-image, as well. As Zig Ziglar put it, "Your attitude, not your aptitude, determines your altitude."

Doing things that make you reach helps you to get ahead and also creates energy and enthusiasm. Break through your barriers as they are self-imposed. Seek greater things. What you "see" is what you get. It is important that we do new and different activities, so we stay enthusiastic. Reward yourself for even small achievements. Try to think outside the box as this increases your creativity and vision. Give it all you got, but if it isn't working, get off it. If one dream dies, dream another dream. It's good to realize that dreams never become a reality without some degree of risk-taking. John F. Kennedy said, "Those to dare to fail miserably can achieve greatly."

Dare to conceive of greater things for yourself. Act as if it is impossible to fail. Get started and never quit. Realize that if it's going to be, it's up to you. Remember, you can't get to second base with one foot on first. I like what Goethe said about action: "Are you earnest? Seize the very minute; what you can do, or dream you can, begin it; boldness has genius, power, and magic in it. Only engage and then the mind grows heated; begin and then the work will be completed."

We must remember there are really no failures, only lessons. We need to appreciate the growth that resulted from the failed experience…so drop the loss and take the gain realizing that nothing is ever a total loss. There is always some gain and growth. It is essential we learn to bounce back from disappointments and apparent defeats quickly. Persistence and perseverance will win eventually. Roger Bannister, the first person to run the four-minute mile said, "The man who can drive himself further once the effort gets painful is the man who will win."

The decisions you make determine your destiny. It is vital we learn to make decisions quickly. It makes achievement more likely as your thinking is crystalized and clarified. Decision making creates action. Charles "Tremendous" Jones hit the nail on the head when he said, "Don't worry about making right decisions; make a decision and work to make it right."

It is helpful to create a daily "to do" list and then check off each accomplishment. This gives you a successful experience and increases your faith in your ability to do what you say you are going to do. It also increases your energy to do greater things because you set a goal and worked toward that goal to help fulfill your mission, talent and destiny.

"The great thing in the world is not so much where we stand, as in what direction we are moving."
-Oliver Wendell Holmes

"Act as if you are, and you will become such."
-Leo Tolstoy

TAKEAWAY: YOU CAN ALWAYS DO MORE AND BE BETTER.

"God has given man the power to create his experience by means of his imagination; therefore, whatever he can see himself being, doing and having in his imagination, he can be, do and have in his experience." -Reverend Ike

"If you can see it in your mind, you can hold it in your hand."-Steve Harvey

7

WHAT YOU "SEE" IS WHAT YOU GET

Visualization is a technique in which you use your imagination to create a clear picture in your mind of whatever you want to create in your life. Visualization is the ability to see things as if they had already happened. You must see it in your mind before you can see it in reality. Our subconscious mind cannot tell the difference between an actual image or one that we run mentally in our minds.

Olympic athletes are known for practicing their routines perfectly in their minds before the actual performance. The more vivid the mental images and the more frequently they are performed, with faith and enthusiasm, the greater the subconscious mind is programmed to manifest the desired result. If you do it right in simulation, you will do it right in reality.

Everything that has been created or invented was once a thought image in the mind of God or in the mind of man. Visualization is a powerful and effective way to help program your mind. Consider the words of Henry David Thoreau, "If one advances confidently in the direction of his dreams, and in endeavors to live the life which he has imagined, he will meet with success unexpected in common hours." Visualize what you intend to achieve, see yourself acting confident, motivated, and enthusiastic. Know you will attract into your life all the people, conditions, and circumstances to fulfill your destiny. Napoleon Hill put it this way, "Hold a picture of yourself long and steadily enough in your mind's eye, and you will be drawn towards it." Man thinks in pictures, and we tend to get what we visualize. What you see is what you get. The more vivid you make your mental images and the more frequently you see them, the quicker you will manifest the desired result.

James Allen observed, "Dream lofty dreams, and as you dream, so shall you become. Your vision is the promise of what you shall one day be; your ideal is the prophecy of what you shall at last unveil." Suzanne Sommers had this to say, "Visualization is powerful. You can use the process to mend your heart, or a sore elbow. I have used visualization as a tool for a successful career for years. I see myself doing what it is that I want, and I do not let go of this picture until it manifests."

An effective way to use visualization is to go someplace where you will not be disturbed, sit in a comfortable chair, close your eyes, and relax. "See" in your mind's eye, the thing or condition or event you want just as you would like it to be. Saying affirmations will support your image. Feel like you have achieved what you desire and give thanks. Repeat your visualization frequently, either in the morning or prior to going to bed. Frederick Pierce thought visualization techniques worked best at bedtime. He said, "Five minutes, just before going to sleep, given to a bit of directed imagination regarding achievement possibilities of the morrow, will steadily and increasingly bear fruit, particularly if all areas of difficulty, worry or fear are resolutely ruled out and replaced by those of accomplishment and smiling courage."

Your subconscious mind will magnify and increase whatever you give your attention to. You will attract into your life what you see in your mind's eye. What you see in your vision becomes your life. It has been said that everything has been created twice – once in the mind and then in reality. Visualization techniques improve the quality of our lives. We need to visualize our day as we'd like it to be. Do this day after day and you will live the life you've imagined. I believe Paul Meyer said it best: "Whatever you vividly imagine, ardently desire, sincerely believe, and enthusiastically act upon, must inevitably come to pass."

"Where there is no vision, the people perish." (Proverbs 29:18)

"I believe that visualization is one of the most powerful means of achieving personal goals."
-Harvey MacKay

"The only thing worse than being blind is having sight but no vision."
-Helen Keller

"It is through the imagination that the formless takes form."
-Catherine Ponder

TAKEAWAY: MAN RECEIVES WHAT HE SEES HIMSELF RECEIVING.

"Definiteness of purpose is the starting point of all achievements." –W. Clement Stone

"Gardens are not made by singing 'Oh, How Beautiful', and sitting in the shade."
–Rudyard Kipling

"A man must sit in a chair with mouth open very long time for roast duck to fly in."
–Chinese Proverb

8

OUR PURPOSE DETERMINES OUR GOALS AND OUR DESTINY

Purpose is something one attempts to get or to do. The purpose of life is to have a life of purpose. Our purpose must be big otherwise problems appear insurmountable. The bigger your purpose, the less problems bother you. It is important that we never let rejection or failure interfere with our purpose. If you become off purpose, you tend to wallow in negativity. A great purpose will inspire us and take us toward our goals. In fact, if a life is not purposeful, we will not have any worthwhile goals. We need to be goal oriented and purpose will take us there. A sense of purpose gives our life meaning. It takes great discipline to stay on purpose. Napoleon Hill wrote, "There is one quality which one must possess to win, and that is definiteness of purpose, the knowledge of what one wants, and a burning desire to possess it." Denis Waitley put it like this, "Winners are people who have a definite purpose in life. No man or woman is an island. To exist just for yourself is meaningless. You can achieve the most satisfaction when you feel related to some greater purpose in life, something greater than yourself." A sense of purpose adds to our happiness and contentment in life. A strong purpose will take you toward your goals and determines the results you will get. Do you think Billy Graham had sense of purpose? Reverend Bob Harrington, the chaplain of Bourbon Street said, "We need a faith to live by, a self to live with, and a purpose to live for."

We must become clear on the things we want and a strong sense of purpose provides that. Its easy to tell when you're not on purpose as you start to major on minor things. Not having fun at work, boredom, fatigue, stress, and seriousness are early signs. A bad attitude is another. You are definitely off purpose and in trouble if you start drinking, gambling, getting involved in extra-marital affairs or using drugs. You must not let pain or pleasure interfere with your purpose.

Whatever your purpose is, you must set goals. A goal is a target — something you wish to have or accomplish. It is a blueprint for action and determines your future. Every person must have goals to keep him from despair. I like what Harvey MacKay had to say about goals: "A dream is just a dream. But a goal is a dream with a plan and a deadline." To the degree that you lack goals is the degree that you will fail. Setting goals gives you energy and direction. It has been said that man may not always achieve his goals, but goals make the man. Tony Robbins said, "Setting goals is the first step in turning the invisible into the visible." A goal is not really a goal until it is written down with a timetable for its achievement. Only 3% of people do this. Some authorities say that a written goal is 50 times more likely to be obtained than one which is not written down. When you write your goals down you are really making a commitment. Dr. Allen Sipes said, "Writing goals crystalizes our thinking and helps to define them." By writing goals down and verbalizing them repeatedly, they are implanted into our subconscious mind. Our goals are first visualized before they are realized.

It's important for each of us to have multiple goals as this creates excitement so we set more and bigger goals. Your fire comes back with big goals. Mark Victor Hanson said he has 6,000 goals! Goals should be set for all areas of life: physical, mental, spiritual, social, financial, and family. We need to have daily, weekly, monthly and lifetime goals. It's good to review your goals frequently and modify them as necessary. It is also vitally important to put a time limit on achieving your goals. It tells the subconscious mind you mean business. A young couple was in the process of moving into a new home when they discovered a piece of paper which had fallen behind the refrigerator. To their amazement, the piece of paper listed 19 goals they had written down together nearly a decade prior and of the 19 goals, 18 had already come to pass.

"People with goals succeed because they know where they are going."
-Earl Nightingale

"Most people don't know what they want in life…but they are sure they haven't gotten it yet."
-Alfred E. Newman

"To be 'on purpose' means you're doing what you love to do, doing what you're good at, and accomplishing what's important to you."
-Jack Canfield

TAKEAWAY: YOUR LIFE IS NOT PURPOSEFUL IF IT'S NOT GOAL ORIENTED.

"If a man neglects education he walks lame to the end of his life."-Plato

"A house without books is like a room without windows."-Horace Mann

9

SCHOOL IS NEVER OUT FOR THE PRO

One year from now, you'll be the same person you are today except for the books you read, the courses you take and the people you meet. It is important we continue to learn throughout our life. The road of life should always be under construction. The purpose of life is to grow so continued study is essential. You are going to be another year older in another year so you might as well be another year better. A few years ago, we had our 50th high school class reunion. It was fun to visit with those folks who have bettered themselves over the past 50 years, while others didn't seem to have changed at all from their high school days. They say that only about 3% of the people read a book in a year. Your formal schooling may be over but that does not mean you're learning shouldn't continue. We can't get so busy chopping wood that we forget to sharpen our ax. Ralph Ingersoll wrote, "Learn to love good books. There are treasures in books that all the money in the world cannot buy, but the poorest laborer can have for nothing." In a similar vein, William Godwin reminds us,, "He that loves reading, has everything within his reach." Some folks recommend underlining important passages so that you can review the book in a matter of minutes to increase your retention. It's always good to have a stack of books you look forward to reading. Reading tends to broaden one's perspective. You become more open minded about people, places, and things. Aristotle said, "It is the mark of an educated mind to be able to entertain a thought without accepting it." Sir Richard Steele said, "Reading is to the mind what exercise is to the body." If we don't continue to learn, our mind starts to stagnate. Mark Twain said, "The man who does not read good books has no advantage over the man who can't read them." And Henry Ford said, "Anyone who stops learning is old, whether at twenty or eighty. Anyone who keeps learning is young." They say the mind expanded to the dimensions of a new idea can never return to its former size. Curiosity is the key to learning.

We are never too old to learn. Aeschylus said, "To learn is to be young, however old." Michelangelo said he was still learning at age 87. Intellectual growth should continue throughout life and cease only at death. We always have room to improve. Learning increases curiosity and curiosity leads to even more learning. Education is a journey, not a destination. One of the greatest values of continuing education is that the parents act as an example to the children in the home. Observing parents reading and having books available encourages youngsters to read and learn, as well. Consider these words from Leo Buscaglia: "The best students come from homes where education is revered: where there are books, and the children see their parents reading them."

Attending seminars is a good way to continue your education as you gain new information and ideas but you also mingle with new people and get to hear various speakers. You can also take college courses at home on the computer or on campus. You can take college level courses from "The Great Courses" and study various courses such as "The Secrets of Mental Math" to "Optimizing Brain Fitness" and practically any subject in between. CDs and audio books are available for minimal cost and are wonderful learning tools. You can listen to audiobooks while driving and learn without effect thus making better use of your traveling time. It's like having a classroom on wheels. Brian Tracy said, "Commit yourself to lifelong learning. The most valuable asset you'll ever have is your mind and what you put into it." Invest in yourself; develop a passion for learning.

"The person who stops studying
merely because he has finished school
is forever hopelessly doomed to
mediocrity, no matter what may be his
calling. The way of success is the
way of continuous pursuit of knowledge."
Napoleon Hill

"The more that you read,
the more things that you will
know. The more that you learn,
the more places that you'll go."
Dr. Seuss

"The illiterate of the 21st century will not be those who cannot read and write but those who cannot learn, unlearn and relearn."
Alvin Toffler

"The recipe for perpetual ignorance is: Be satisfied with your opinions and content with your knowledge."
Elbert Hubbard

"Once you stop learning, you start dying."
Albert Einstein

TAKEAWAY:
YOUR SCHOOLING MAY BE OVER BUT YOUR EDUCATION MUST CONTINUE FOR THE REST OF YOUR LIFE

"What we feed our minds is even more important than what we feed our bodies." -Ed Foreman

"People often say that motivation doesn't last. Well, neither does bathing — that's why we recommend it daily."-Zig Ziglar

10

DAILY DOSES OF MOTIVATION AND INSPIRATION ARE NEEDED

When it comes to motivation and inspiration, we have to depend on ourselves as no one else can do it for us. You have to motivate and inspire yourself daily with pep talks. If you learn to talk yourself up, nobody else will be able to talk you down. Everyone must protect themselves from mass mind negativity which is so prevalent today. It is impossible for anyone to live a happy, productive and serene life by watching television or listening to negativity on the radio. If you watch the news or read the newspaper before work, you are halfway to a bad day before you even get to work. Emmet Fox said, "You must not under any pretense allow your mind to dwell on any thought that is not positive, constructive, optimistic, kind."

In order to stay motivated and inspired we must avoid toxic people…those that are always sick and love to tell you about it, those who grumble and complain about everything and those who are always negative, etc.

Motivation and inspiration are like nutrition; we need daily doses to help keep us pumped up and excited about life, otherwise we will become fatigued and deflated which leads to hopelessness, despair and finally, depression. Even something as simple as looking into the mirror and saying something positive to yourself such as, "You're looking good, girl," is helpful. What you tell yourself will determine how far you'll go and long it will take to get there. The words we speak, both to ourselves and to others, weave a deep impression on our subconscious mind so we must continually monitor our speech and self-talk. Our minds are like a computer…if you put garbage in, you get garbage out. It is extremely important we become aware of our habitual thinking and the words we say to ourselves (self-talk) and others as our subconscious mind records everything. What we say makes a huge difference; what you say is what you get. Louise Hay put it like this, "We create our experiences by our thoughts and words." Sometimes we forget and utter a negative statement such as, "I've got a bad back" or "That makes me sick." When that happens it's good to say, "Cancel" and then replace the negative statement with a positive one. This helps us get back on track and we tend to become aware of our negative self-talk. A good affirmation is, "I monitor my words and keep them positive."

Positive self-talk helps to improve our mental, physical, emotional, and spiritual health. It helps us to view the world more favorably and improves our confidence and performance and makes us feel good about ourselves. Some authorities even say an optimistic dialogue with ourselves improves our resistance to infectious diseases. Positive self-talk helps us to feel good physically, as well. A claimed author of inspirational books, Ruth Fishel, writes: "Brain wave tests prove that when we use positive words, 'our feel good' hormones flow. Positive self-talk releases endorphins and serotonin in our brain which then flows throughout our body, making us feel good. These neurotransmitters stop flowing when we use negative words." Cortisol, a stress hormone, becomes elevated with stressful conditions and negative self-talk. A positive self-dialogue helps with stress management and lowers depression rates, as well. The bottom line is if you want to change your life experiences, you must change the way you talk.

Daily affirmations are helpful tools to influence our mind favorably. An affirmation means to validate or confirm. The purpose of affirmations is to condition your mind positively to reduce negative beliefs. Affirmations build you up and strengthen you. Some folks refer to this as auto-suggestion or self-talk. These are positive statements a person makes to himself which are repeated frequently until the subconscious mind accepts what you are saying as fact. By using affirmations, you will improve your self-image and you will become more effective in your work and in your dealings with others. Denis Waitley said, "Relentless, repetitive self-talk is what changes our self-image." A similar statement by W. Clement Stone is as follows, "Self-suggestion makes you master of yourself." Daily affirmations are more effective if repeated early in the morning or just before bedtime. Some examples of positive affirmations include the following:

Every day in every way, I am on my way!
I'm alive. I'm alert. I feel great!
I choose to be happy today!
I am unbelievably blessed!
I am under the influence of divine wisdom!
"I feel good. I feel great. I feel terrific!" (Ed Foreman)

You can create your own affirmations. Try to create some that make a deep impression on you. Years ago, Émile Coué helped thousands of people regain their health by having them repeat the following, "Everyday in every way, I am getting better and better." Grenville Kleiser provided this insight, "You can vitally influence your life from within by auto suggestion. The first thing each morning, and the last thing each night, suggest to yourself specific ideas that you wish to embody in your character and personality. Address such suggestions to yourself, privately or aloud, until they are deeply impressed upon your mind."

Another effective way to inspire and motivate yourself is to get into the habit of visualizing what you want to see happen in your life. Visualization is a process of running motion pictures over and over in your mind. Since our minds cannot tell the difference between an actual experience and an imagined experience, visualization is extremely effective. Suppose you would like to take a trip to Hawaii. Close your eyes, relax, and try to imagine how excited you are as the big day of departure approaches. Emotionalize this as much as possible as it makes a greater impression on your subconscious mind. "Hear" the sounds of the surf, "feel" the warm sand beneath your feet and between your toes, "feel" the cool water on your feet and legs as you walk in the ocean and "feel" the trade winds on your face as you watch a breathtaking sunrise or sunset." The more details you can make your visualization, the more effective it will be. Another good technique is to create multiple vision boards and display them in various places. This allows you to see and be motivated by them frequently. For example, you could have a vision board with multiple pictures of Hawaii and the activities you wish to do while there.

Listening to CDs and tapes and watching videos help to provide daily doses of inspiration and motivation. We can listen to positive messages while we drive to and from work, which is a lot better than listening to the negative news on the radio. What we say to ourselves and what we watch and listen to makes a huge difference in our life. People tend to quit if they run out of motivation. We all need encouragement. As Charles 'Tremendous' Jones said, "Encouragement is oxygen for the soul."

It is best to remember that inspiration and motivation is useless unless we take action. A change in thinking can change our behavior and our outcomes…but only if we act.

"By your words you will be justified, and by your words you will be condemned." -(Matthew 12:37)

"Hush! Check those words. Do not cure ill with ill and make your pain still heavier than it is." -Sophocles

VISION WITHOUT ACTION
is merely a dream
ACTION WITHOUT VISION
just passes the time.
VISION WITH ACTION
can change the world.
Joel A. Barker

TAKEAWAY: WE MUST MOTIVATE OURSELVES TO BE OUR BEST.

Dr. Myren D. Anderson

"You can exist without work, but you can't live without work" -Charles Tremendous Jones

"Work gives you meaning and purpose and life is empty without it." -Stephen Hawking

11

THE JOY OF WORK

Work allows us to achieve our mission, talent and destiny. It gives purpose to our lives. We work, not just to get our daily bread, clothes and shelter, but to create a life. Work allows us to grow as individuals and growth is what life is all about. Begin to think of your work as a calling. Feel like God chose you to do the job you are doing. Let your work become a labor of love and always go the "extra mile". Rumi hit the nail on the head when he said, "Everyone has been made for some particular work, and the desire for that work has been put in every heart." Always see yourself as being in the right place, at the right time with the right people, doing the right job.

If we love our work, it really doesn't seem like work because we get into flow and time passes quickly. Joy comes because of the satisfaction we get for doing a good job, especially if it was difficult and demanded our best effort. Confucius observed, "Choose a job you love, and you'll never have to work a day in your life." Let your work become a labor of love and put your heart into it. Do your work for the love of it. Make sure you are not only working for a paycheck. Work should be challenging and enjoyable. If it is not, you are merely a slave. Six out of 10 people hate to go to work every day. You cannot fulfill your mission, talent and destiny doing work you despise. Malcom Forbes said, "The biggest mistake people make is not making a living and doing what they most enjoy." So, if you are unhappy with your job, try to find one you are happy with. The quality of your life largely depends on your work and the satisfaction and pride you feel from having done your best.

There is work to do and somebody needs to do it. An old German proverb says, "God gives us nuts, but he does not crack them." One of the greatest benefits of work is that when we are working, we don't tend to think about our troubles. Eleanor Roosevelt observed: "My experience has been that work is almost the best way to pull oneself out of the depths."

One of the benefits of working is the sense of fulfillment one feels when he is contributing to the welfare of others. Get inspired. Thank God that you're able to work. It seems like a lot of work is done by those who are tired, or busy, or not feeling well. They tend to lose themselves in their work. Many times, work tends to lift one's spirit and helps to keep us on an even keel. This is particularly true when we are working in service to others. There is no greater thrill than to help someone enjoy their life more. You feel like you have been blessed twice — once for the opportunity to serve and once for the rewards of service whether it be for a smile, a paycheck or an inner knowing that you were of service to one of God's children. Mother Teresa said, "Let us touch the dying, the poor, the lonely and the unwanted according to the graces we have received and let us not be ashamed or slow to do the humble work." Indeed, service to others is a privilege and is deeply rewarding. I believe the true measure of a man is the number of people he serves.

Working gives us a platform to better our best and to strive for excellence. We must always perform our duties to the very best of our abilities. Therefore, we should strive to do our work in the spirit of an artist. Excellence is our own reward. Doing a job well nourishes the ego and the spirit and it gives us a successful experience. Doing our best increases our enthusiasm for our work and it helps us to overcome boredom and fatigue. Having fun and doing a job enthusiastically will allow you to enjoy your work more and you'll do a better job in the long run. As Aristotle said, "Pleasure in the job puts perfection in the work."

Work helps to keep us happy. One of the wisest of men, Benjamin Franklin said, "It is the working man who is the happy man. It is the idle man who is miserable." The person who works is a giver not a taker. He gets self-worth and satisfaction for doing an honest day's work. This is not true for those who do not work. They have no special purpose to fulfill; they are just existing. Work is more than just making a living, as vital as that is. It is fundamental to human dignity, to our sense of self-worth and fulfillment. Think of your work as an opportunity to make a life.

Working helps us stay young as we tend to learn something new each day. Work keeps us active in mind and body. It gives us a purpose to live for each day and a reason to wake up every morning. It is those small daily happenings that make life so well worth living. Pearl S. Buck said it very well: "To find joy in work is to discover the foundation of youth." Work makes us feel alive; it makes us feel like we are riding the crest of the wave. Working helps you to fill your days with fun and meaningful activities. We all need obstacles to conquer and goals to achieve which work provides. As Robert Louis Stevenson summed it up so beautifully, "The best things are nearest: breath in your nostrils, light in your eyes, flowers at your feet, duties at your hand, the path of God just before you. Then do not grasp at the stars, but do life's plain, common work as it comes, certain that daily duties and daily bread are the sweetest things in life."

There is something about work that helps people live longer as well. There is an old adage that says, "Retire and expire." It seems many people die shortly after retiring, usually within three years. Some live a while after retirement but never stop missing their work. They may have a few hobbies, but it is not enough to keep them going. If a person retires, it is absolutely vital they get a part-time job or at least volunteer their services to some worthy cause frequently. Your mental faculties will diminish, and your body will deteriorate faster if not used. If you don't use it, you will lose it. Work keeps people physically active, socially connected and mentally challenged. Geriatrician Katherine Schlaerth said, "Most people just plain do better, both intellectually and physically, when they continue to work." Don't let entropy set in prematurely. Continue to work; continue to live. Two hundred plus years ago, Voltaire wrote, "Work keeps us from three great evils — boredom, vice and want." Work is great therapy and helps you to gather your second wind.

Most folks look forward to retirement with great anticipation. When they retire, everything is good for a while. They get to sleep in, play golf, travel, hunt, and fish. But soon they realize that it's an empty life and depression sets in, and the downward spiral develops. As Ezra Taft Benson, former secretary of agriculture said, "Retirement from work has depressed many a man and hastened his death." Here's what Walter Cronkite, anchorman for CBS news for 19 years, had to say about his retirement, "I want to say that probably 24 hours after I told CBS that I was stepping down at my 65th birthday, I was already regretting it. And I regretted it ever since." Hugh Heffner offers us his wisdom, "I think that retirement is the first step towards the grave."

Look at your work in terms of the privilege it gives you to grow as a person. Work keeps us going and gives satisfaction and pleasure and we need to embrace it enthusiastically and wholeheartedly. A sage of old said many years ago, "If you want to leave footprints in the sands of time, wear work shoes." Perhaps, retirement is an idea whose time has come and gone.

I believe we need to take frequent vacations and long weekends to prevent overload on our nervous system (burnout). The perfect combination of work and play will help to keep one young and enthusiastic. There is a time to fish…and a time to dry your nets. Consider the words of Sydney J. Harris, "Work and play are an artificial pair of opposites because the best kind of play contains an element of work, and the most productive type of work must include something of the spirit of play." Consider your work as play and have fun doing it. Enjoy your challenges while working and your leisure time when you're not working.

Dr. Myren D. Anderson

"God honors people who work.
That's the difference between free enterprise and free loaders."
-Reverend Bob Harrington

"As a day well spent procures a happy sleep, so a
life well employed procures a happy death."
-Leonardo DaVinci

"Thank God every morning when you get up that you have something to do that day which must be done, whether you like it or not. Being forced to work, and forced to do your best, will breed in you temperance and self-control, diligence and strength of will, cheerfulness and content, and a hundred virtues which the idle never know." -Charles Kingsley

"Employment is nature's physician and is essential to human happiness."-Galen

"If a man is called to be a street sweeper, he should sweep streets even as a Michelangelo painted, or Beethoven composed music or Shakespeare wrote poetry. He should sweep streets so well that all the hosts of heaven and earth will pause to say, "Here lived a great street sweeper who did his job well." -Martin Luther King Jr.

If You Want To Be Happy
If you want to be happy for one hour…take a nap, for one day…go fishing, for one week…take a trip, for one month…get married, for one year…inherit a fortune, for a life…love your work.
-Anonymous

TAKEAWAY: WORK IS ESSENTIAL FOR A HAPPY LIFE.

"Most men fail, not through lack of education, but from lack of dogged determination, from lack of dauntless will." –Orison Swett Marden

"This man Wellington is so stupid he does not know when he is beaten and goes on fighting."
–Napoleon Bonaparte

12

WINNERS NEVER QUIT; QUITTERS NEVER WIN

To win, we must persevere and never give up. We need to keep on keeping on with tenacity. To persevere is to continue to do something in spite of difficulty. It's getting up six times after being knocked down six times. As Ralph Waldo Emerson said, "Our greatest glory consists not in never failing but in rising every time we fall." The disgrace in life is not in falling down but in not getting back up. It's realizing that "this too shall pass" during the dark days. Victory over challenges and obstacles enhances our self-image and improves the quality of our life. Learn to bounce back from apparent defeats quickly and do things that make you reach. Know that God's delays are not God's denials. If at first, you do not succeed, try again and again. Columbus said, "Sail on, sail on, sail on and on." With perseverance a person keeps trying until he succeeds. The tide always turns. Congratulate yourself on how much you have already accomplished. Keep your eye on your goals, otherwise all you see are obstacles. Perseverance keeps you going. I like what the great pitcher Cy Young said, "In our day, when a pitcher got into trouble in a game, instead of taking him out, our manager would leave him in and tell him to pitch his way out of trouble."

Winners make goals and work hard to achieve them. You wouldn't play football without a goal line but many people will go through their whole lives without setting any worthwhile goals. Goals help us to keep on track and inspire us to do better. Charles C. Noble offers this wisdom, "You must have long-range goals to keep you from being frustrated by short-range failures." If you set incredible goals, you will achieve incredible results. Get started…and never quit.

Obstacles are those daunting things you see when you take your mind off your goals. If we fail at a task we must persevere and try again. The great inventor Thomas A. Edison reminds us, "Many of life's failures are men who did not realize how close they were to success when they gave up." Josh Billings said, "Be like a postage stamp-stick to one thing until you get there." Elbert Hubbard had this advice: "The line between failure and success is so fine that we…are often on the line and do not know it. How many a man has thrown up his hands at a time when a little more effort, a little more patience, would have achieved success. A little more persistence, a little more effort, and what seemed hopeless failure may turn to glorious success." Persistence is the absolute refusal to give up. Calvin Coolidge didn't say a lot, in fact he was called "Silent Cal," but he had this to say about persistence: "Nothing in the world can take place of persistence. Talent will not; nothing is more common than unsuccessful individuals with talent. Genius will not; unrewarded genius is almost a proverb. Education will not; the world is full of educated derelicts. Persistence and determination alone are omnipotent."

And who can forget Winston Churchill's immortal words during the Battle of Britain in World War II: "We shall not flag or fail. We shall go on to the end. We shall fight in France, we shall fight on the seas and the oceans, we shall fight with growing confidence and growing strength in the air, we shall defend our island, whatever the cost may be. We shall fight on the beaches, we shall fight on the landing grounds, we shall fight in the fields and in the streets, we shall fight in the hills; we shall never surrender." Winston Churchill changed the world forever. If not for him peoples of the world would be speaking German and the entire world would be enslaved by the Nazis. To achieve success in any endeavor, whether it's raising a family or running a business, an individual must have unwavering perseverance. The job must go on regardless of difficulties and challenges. Success without conflict is unrealistic. God put stumbling blocks so they would become stepping stones. See yourself doing what you want to do and having what you want to have. Don't just do enough to get by; do enough to get ahead. You are either all in or not. Rekindle your purpose. Your purpose must be strong and will determine the results you get. Your purpose will take you towards your goals regardless of obstacles. Say to yourself, "I am the master of persistence. I will not quit."

The following poem by an unknown author says it all:

Don't Quit
When things wrong, as they sometimes will,
When the road you're trudging seems all uphill,
When the funds are low and the debts are high,
And you want to smile, but you have to sigh,
When care is pressing you down a bit-
Rest if you must, but don't you quit.

Life is queer with its twists and turns,
As everyone of us sometimes learns
And many a fellow-turns about
When he might have won had he stuck it out.

Don't give up though the pace seems slow-
You may succeed with another blow.

Often the goal is nearer than
It seems to a faint and faltering man;
Often the struggler has given up
When he might have captured the victor's cup;
And he learned too late when the night came down,
How close he was to the golden crown.

Success is failure turned inside out-
The silver tint of the clouds of doubt,
And you never can tell how close you are,
It may be near when it seems afar;
So, stick to the fight when you're hardest hit,
It's when things seem worst that you mustn't quit.

"Whatsoever thy hand findeth to do, do it with all thy might."
(Ecclesiastes 9-10)

"Defeat doesn't finish
a man, quit does.
A man is not finished
when he is defeated.
He's finished
when he quits."

Richard M. Nixon
American President 1913-1994

"By perseverance the snail reached the ark."
-Charles Haddon Spurgeon

"Never give in! Never give in!
Never, never, never, never…in
nothing great or small, large or petty,
never give in except to convictions
or honor and good sense!"
-Winston Churchill

TAKEAWAY: YOU CAN'T EVER WIN IF YOU GIVE UP

Dr. Myren D. Anderson

"To make no mistakes is not in the power of man; but from their errors and mistakes the wise and good learn wisdom for the future." –Plutarch

"Failure is the foundation of success, and the means by which it is achieved."– Lao Tzu

13

THERE ARE NO FAILURES OR MISTAKES, ONLY LESSONS

In any worthwhile endeavor, it is likely you will make a few mistakes or experience failure along the way. Sometimes you will fail to get the result you want, and you'll suffer a setback. Setbacks can be learning experiences and usually pave the way for comebacks. It is imperative that we anticipate the good even during the bad. Many times, mistakes and failures occur so that we can define and redefine our efforts and go on to greater good. You always learn something from mistakes and setbacks. If it doesn't turn out exactly as you expected, move on. Past failures have made you wiser and stronger than you would have been without the benefit of that experience. Perhaps you have learned another way that will work. They say that good judgment comes from experiences, and a lot of that comes from bad judgment! Learn to laugh at yourself if you made a silly mistake. Forgive yourself if you fail but keep on trying. Never fear that you will make a mistake, and if you make one, never brood over it. Never dwell on your mistakes or failures. This will cause you to condemn yourself unjustly. This will kill future initiatives and ensure that you fail permanently.

Many times, we attempt projects which are beyond our present abilities. Just because we have failed doesn't mean that the whole project was a total loss or a bad idea. Now we know what didn't work and the resulting experience will give us new insights into what might work. Thoreau said, "If you have built castles in the air, your work need not be lost; that is where they should be. Now put the foundations under them."

James Reston spoke about life's failures and defeats: "One of the advantages of defeat in life, maybe the main advantage, is that it provides an excuse for change. Defeat… invariably leads to new adventures. Great people are never stopped by a temporary defeat. They just look for new ways to make the best of the situation."
Problems, difficulties, and challenges strengthen us by causing us to tap into our inner strength to find power within ourselves. W. Clement Stone wrote, "Like success, failure is many things to many people. With a positive mental attitude, failure is a learning experience, a rung on the ladder, a plateau at which you can get your thoughts in order and prepare to try again." The difficulties in life, such as failures, are meant to make us better. Sometimes God breaks us down to build us up. Failure can help us grow. All experiences are valuable. So, in reality, failure is not all bad as there can be positives that arise from failure. Failure tends to make us stronger and more resilient. It helps us to learn what we need to do to turn things around. If we do not give up, it can eventually lead to success. And lastly, it keeps us humble and prevents us from getting overconfident and cocky.

Jacob M. Braude said, "Life is a grindstone; whether it grinds you down or polishes you up depends on what you're made of." So, let us learn from our mistakes and setbacks, but don't let them become roadblocks. Press on. As this Japanese Proverb says, "Fall seven times, get up eight." Learn the lesson; throw away the experience. When we get up when we're knocked down and when we refuse to accept defeat and failure, we show strength of character and courage. As Robert G. Ingersoll observed: "The greatest test of courage on earth is to bear defeat without losing heart." Winston Churchill said, "Success consists of going from failure to failure without loss of enthusiasm." And he also stated, "Success is not final, failure is not fatal. It is the courage to continue that counts."

There is probably no greater joy in life than finally succeeding after many failed efforts as it tends to justify our efforts and brightens our soul. As Truman Capote put it, "Failure is the condiment that gives success its flavor." We also need to accept things as they come because what you wanted might not have been for your greater good. As Rumi said, "Don't grieve for what doesn't come. Some things that don't happen keep disasters from happening." So, drop the loss (failure) and take the gain (experience). With every failure there is always some good, so go forth with faith and expectancy and keep on keeping on. Put your attention on wins not losses and move on.

"The credit belongs to the man who is actually in the arena; whose face is marred by dust and sweat and blood; who strives valiantly; who errs and comes short again and again; who knows the great enthusiasms, the great devotions, and spends himself in a worthy cause; who, at the worst, if he fails, at least fails while daring greatly, so that his place shall never be with those cold and timid souls who know neither victory nor defeat." -Theodore Roosevelt

"I have not failed. I've just found 10,000 ways that won't work." -Thomas A. Edison

TAKEAWAY: THINK OF FAILURE AS A LESSON LEARNED

"Defensive strategy never has produced ultimate victory."-General Douglas MacArthur

"Unless you enter the tiger's den, you cannot take the cubs."-Japanese Proverb

14

RISK TAKING IS ESSENTIAL FOR SUCCESS

If you want to have success, health and happiness in this life we must take risks. As David Viscot said, "If your life is ever to get better, you have to take risks. There is simply no way you can grow without taking chances." So, make it okay to take risks…even if you make mistakes. Learn what you can from every experience. If you make a mistake, correct it and move on.

Make it a rule to always try for more…act one step bigger than you feel. Push yourself beyond your comfort zone. Go out on a limb if necessary; that is where the fruit is. If you want different results you will need to make different choices. As Jim Rohn said, "If you're not willing to risk the unusual, you will have to settle for the ordinary." If you are averse to risk, you will never reach your full potential. There is a tendency for people to "play it safe" and to not "rock the boat." For example, many times the prettiest girl has the fewest dates because most guys are intimidated and don't take a chance by asking her for a date. As Ralph Waldo Emerson put it, "Don't be too timid and squeamish…all life is an experiment. The more experiments you make, the better." It is better to attempt something great and to fail than to do nothing and succeed. Don't wait for everything to be perfect; jump in.

They say that ships are safest in the harbor but that's not what ships are made for. It may be that a policy of being too cautious and doing nothing is the greatest risk of all. Any goal worth achieving involves an element of risk. Consider the wisdom of Maxwell Maltz, "Often the difference between a successful man and a failure is not one's better abilities or ideas, but the courage that one has to bet on his ideas, to take a calculated risk, and to act."

If we don't try to do great things we'll never know if greatness is within us. I like T.S. Elliot's observation, "Only those who risk going too far can possibly find out how far one can go." You can't get ahead at all if you don't take a chance. General George Patton said, "Take calculated risks…that is quite different from being rash." Life is sweetened by taking risks. Not only will risk taking assure you more success, it will eliminate boredom from your life and will add an element of excitement and positive expectations. Unless you are willing to take the risk, you'll never get the reward.

When we get to the end of our life, we don't want to have regrets about what we didn't do. Perhaps, we had an interest in politics early on and now we're sorry because we didn't try for state legislature or Congress. Many people have stayed for 40 years in a job they despise while all that time he or she was thinking how nice it would be if they could run an orchard or small farm, something they truly loved. As Helen Rowland said, "The follies which a man regrets most in his life are those which he didn't commit when he had the opportunity." You'll never know how far you can go unless you take a chance and go for it. As Shakespeare summed it up so beautifully, "We know what we are, but know not what we may be." There wouldn't be any progress at all unless man took risks. Dreams would never become a reality without risk and how much one is willing to fail determines the amount of success achieved. Progress always involves risks. I quote Brooks Atkinson, "This nation was built by men who took risks-pioneers who were not afraid of the wilderness, businessmen who were not afraid of failure, scientists who were not afraid of the truth, thinkers who were not afraid of progress, dreamers who were not afraid of actions."

I came across this poem quoted in "Dear Abby" and I believe it says it all.

> To laugh is to risk appearing the fool.
> To weep is to risk appearing sentimental.
> To reach for another is to risk involvement.
> To expose your ideas, your dreams,
> before a crowd, is to risk their loss.
> To love is to risk not being loved in return.
> To live is to risk dying.
> To believe is to risk failure.
> But risks must be taken, because the
> greatest hazard in life is to risk nothing.
> The people who risk nothing do
> nothing, have nothing, are nothing.
> They may avoid suffering and sorrow, but they cannot learn, feel,
> change, grow, love, live.
> Chained by their attitudes, they are
> slaves; they have forfeited their
> freedom.
> Only a person who risks is free.

"Do not be like the cat who wanted a fish but was afraid to get his paws wet." -William Shakespeare

"A smooth sea never made a skillful mariner."
English Proverb

TAKEAWAY: RISK TAKING IS NECESSARY TO ACHIEVE ANYTHING WORTH WHILE.

"Never cut a tree down in the wintertime. Never make a negative decision in a low time. Never make your most important decisions when you are in your worst moods. Wait. Be Patient. The storm will pass. The spring will come."
–Robert H. Schuller

"The lesson I strive to learn, the lesson which appears so easy, but is so hard, is to remember in the down times that they will not last and the up times will return." –Gamaliel Bradford

15

NEVER MAKE A NEGATIVE DECISION IN A "DOWN" TIME

It is extremely important we never make a negative decision when we are feeling low, especially if you are contemplating quitting something or giving up on a project or relationship. Our moods change…sometimes we are at the top of the world and other times we may be melancholy or even depressed. It is during our low times we should not make major decisions, especially negative ones, as they have the potential to affect us adversely in the future. Remember, the tide always comes back. Down times are followed by up times. It is the nature of the universe to change and so it is with our emotions. So, if you are a bit down, wait to make your decisions so they can be made rationally at a later date.

When we have difficult decisions to make it is helpful to follow Benjamin Franklin's advice, "When comforted with two courses of action I jot down on a piece of paper all the arguments in favor of each one, then on the opposite side I write down the arguments against each one. When by weighing the arguments pro and con and canceling them out, one against the other, I take the course indicated by what remains." This is good advice which has stood the test of time.

We all need to make decisions daily and the more decisive we are the easier our life will be. In order to make good decisions, we need to get all the facts and then act on them. It is always good to set deadlines when making decisions. Always seek your own counsel and never worry about making a mistake. The worst thing we can do in decision making is to procrastinate or to put off the decision indefinitely. People who have difficulty making decisions create a lot of stress for themselves and others. John Foster said it very well, "A man without a decision can never be said to belong to himself; he is as a wave in the sea or a feather in the air which every breeze blows about." Not making a decision is always a wrong decision. Conditions are never perfect for decision making but we will do better if we take the bull by the horns and act. William Feather said, "Conditions are never just right. People who delay action until all factors are favorable do nothing." Decisions should be made quickly and once a decision is made, stick with that decision. Charles "Tremendous" Jones said this, "Don't worry about making right decisions; make a decision and work to make it right." Learning how to make good decisions is a skill that can be learned and will pay huge dividends throughout one's life. The decisions we make determine our destiny. Things happen after decisions are made.

"All my life, whenever it comes time to make a decision, I make it and forget about it."
-Harry S. Truman

"It is in your moments of decision that your destiny is shaped.
-Tony Robbins

TAKEAWAY: MAKE DECISIONS QUICKLY AND STICK WITH THAT DECISION BUT DON'T MAKE ANY IMPORTANT DECISIONS IN A LOW TIME.

Dr. Myren D. Anderson

"I will instruct you and teach you the way you should go." -(Psalms 32:8)

"Anyone who follows the inner leadings of divine wisdom will have a long life, riches, honor, pleasantness, peace of mind, health and happiness." -Solomon

16

TRUST YOUR INTUITION

Our minds are connected to universal intelligence (God) through the subconscious mind which knows all. Universal intelligence created the universe and keeps the planets in orbit. It winged the bird, finned the fish and fanged the beast. It tells your body how to make liver, muscle and other cells from the ham and eggs you had for breakfast, for example. It is the same intelligence that creates a healthy baby boy or girl in nine months' time from a single cell from each parent. When the baby is born there are two holes in the head where the eyes are and two for the ears, etc. The upper teeth always grow down, and the bottom teeth always grow up. Folks call this "nature" but all of nature is controlled by universal intelligence. There is an inborn or innate intelligence within all living things. God speaks to us through little messages called intuition. These are the hunches we have from time to time. Shakti Gawain explains it this way, "There is a universal, intelligent, life force that exists within everyone and everything. It resides within each one of us as a deep wisdom, an inner knowing. We can access this wonderful source of knowledge and wisdom through our intuition, an inner sense that tells us what feels right and true for us at any given moment." When we tap into universal intelligence with our subconscious mind and our intuition, we tap into divine wisdom which knows the perfect answer. A genius is someone who regularly does this. It has been said that the subconscious mind is the womb of creation. God prompts us with little thoughts, ideas, and directives somewhat like a quiet whisper. We need to listen to that inner voice. If a thought persists, take action as it will be right. Intuition means, "taught from within." Be awake to those intuitive leads. Webster's New World Dictionary defines intuition as, "the immediate knowing or learning of something without the conscious use of reasoning." Edgar Cayce had this to say, "Depend more on the intuitive forces from within and not harken so much to outside influences but learn to listen to the still small voice within." We need to take time for silence and meditation. An unknown writer said, "Ignoring your intuition is like going through life blindfolded." Those thoughts and ideas that suddenly pop into your head that encourage you to do something or not to do something is God talking to you. Always be alert to intuitive leads as you are being guided, prompted, and directed. Divine wisdom knows the perfect answer so pay attention and trust your intuition. Learn to make decisions by your gut feeling. It has been said that your gut knows what your head hasn't figured out yet. As you learn to trust your inner feelings, they will become stronger. Never go against your feelings and better judgment or get talked into doing something that doesn't feel right. If it feels wrong, it is probably wrong. Trusting and obeying your intuition can save you from disaster. Infinite mind (God) puts ideas into your mind and words into your mouth and the more you listen to these little prompts, the more they will guide you.

A wonderful technique that helps us connect with universal intelligence is to meditate a few minutes each day. Getting quiet slows down and relaxes our mind. Carlyle said, "Silence is the element in which great things fashioned themselves." Silence allows hunches to enter our mind much more easily. It is a good idea to carry a pen and pad to write down the good ideas that come to you before they disappear.

Diane Robinson said, "Prayer is when you talk to God; meditation is when you listen to God." Prayer is an effective method of increasing your intuitive powers. H. Emily Cady said, "We talk to God… that is prayer; God talks to us…that is inspiration." When you have a problem and pray for guidance, the answer comes and tends to linger in your mind. Florence Shinn wrote, "Intuition is a spiritual facility and does not explain, but simply points the way."

Another technique that many people find useful is to consider a problem and then put it out of your mind. In a few hours or days, the answer will come. Sometimes all you have to do is sleep on it and the answer will be there in the morning. Learning to trust your intuition will change your life. Gisele Bundchen phrased it this way, "The more you trust your intuition, the more empowered you become, the stronger you become and the happier you become." Shakti Gawain said, "Your intuition will tell you where you need to go; it will connect you with people you need to meet; it will guide you towards work that is meaningful to you – work that brings you joy, work that feels right for you."

"The only really valuable thing is intuition."
Albert Einstein

"When I have a problem I pray about it, and what comes to mind and stays there I assume to be my answer. And this has been right so often that I know it is God's answer."
J. L. Kraft

"When your mind is functioning correctly, there is an out streaming of light from within in the form of inspiration, hunches, leadings and intuitive flashes – trust this process of inspiration. In the twinkling of an eye ideas and plans may flow into your mind."
Eric Butterworth

"In a dream, in a
vision of the
night, when deep sleep falleth upon
men, in slumberings upon the bed;
then he openeth the ears of men,
and sealeth their instruction."
Job 33:15-16
King James Bible

TAKEAWAY: TRUST YOUR HUNCHES AND GUT FEELINGS.

"If everyone is thinking alike, then someone isn't thinking."-Gen. George S. Patton (1885-1945)

"Sometimes what worked 40 years ago doesn't work today."-Joel Osteen

17

YESTERDAY'S ANSWER MAY NOT WORK TODAY

For many people, change is difficult as they have become set in their ways and are used to doing things in a certain way and have gotten comfortable in their own comfort zone. The inability to change keeps some people from advancing and destroys others. To advance and prosper in today's world it is vitally important that we change our thinking when necessary. We must anticipate and adapt to changes in life and especially in the marketplace. Great things never come from your comfort zone. Change is occurring very rapidly in all industries.

A good example is the way books are sold today. It used to be about the only place you could buy books was at a bookstore or a store like Walmart or Kmart. Now, many books are sold via the internet and many people read all their books on electronic devices. As a result, many booksellers have gone out of business. Charles F. Kettering had this comment about change, "The whole world hates change, yet it is the only thing that has brought progress." Thomas Carlyle put it this way, "Today is not yesterday; how can our words and thoughts, if they are always to be fittest, continue always the same? Change, indeed, is painful, yet ever needful." Another example of folks who were left behind because they continued to use yesterday's technology in today's world are the small family farmers. They simply could not compete with the large corporate farmers who were able to increase productivity while at the same time decreasing expenses for chemicals, fertilizer, seed, farm labor and interest. George Bernard Shaw said, "Progress is impossible without change, and those who cannot change their minds cannot change anything."

The old saying, "If you do what you've always done, you'll get what you always got" is true. Henry Ford, one of America's greatest industrialists and founder of the Ford Motor Company was slow to change, however. Ford developed the Model T in 1918 and it was a great success until the mid-20s when sales dropped sharply, and he was forced to produce the Model A in 1927. Ford said, "Any customer could have a car painted any color that he wants so long that it is black." Other auto companies offered various colors and added many new features to their overall lineup and even had customer credit plans which Ford opposed until the 1930s. Ford realized he had to change and eventually followed suit and prospered.

Become comfortable with change. You are headed for more change and it will come faster. The nature of the universe is to change. We need to do things differently; what you are doing now may not be working. Do not resist change as success requires continual change. Change is what keeps life exciting. We don't have to reinvent the wheel, only modify it. Melvin B. Tolson said this about change, "Since we live in a changing universe, why do men oppose change? If a rock is in the way, the root of a tree will change its direction. The dumbest animals try to adapt themselves to changed conditions. Even a rat will change its tactics to get a piece of cheese." Yesterday's answers may not work in today's marketplace. Refine, adapt and move forward. Quit doing the same things over and over expecting a different result.

"Life belongs to the living and he who lives must be prepared for changes." -Johann Wolfgang Von Goethe

"Old ways won't open new doors." -Anonymous

"In times of change, learners inherit the earth, while the learned find themselves beautifully equipped to deal with a world that no longer exists." -Eric Hoffer

TAKEAWAY: NEVER RESIST OR FEAR CHANGE. WITHOUT CHANGE, THERE IS NO PROGRESS.

Dr. Myren D. Anderson

"A smooth sea never made a skillful mariner."
-English Proverb

"The gem cannot be polished without friction, nor man perfected without trials."
-Confucius

18

LEARN TO OVERCOME ADVERSITY

Dr. Robert Schuller wrote a marvelous book entitled, "Tough Times Never Last, Tough People Do." In this book, he provided examples of how people suffered hardships and eventually persevered. He also offered practical advice on how to deal with adversity. What happens to an individual is not as important as how one reacts to the situation. Some folks suffer some type of misfortune and they quit on the spot; others pick up the pieces and go on. Some people pray to have easier lives – others pray to be stronger men. Will Rogers said, "The worst thing that happens to you may be the best thing for you if you don't let it get the best of you." Eric Butterworth put it like this, "Things may happen around you, and things may happen to you, but the only things that matter are the things that happen in you." Adversity is common to every person in greater or lesser degrees; a problem free life is an illusion. If you are traveling on the river of life, it is likely you will hit a few rocks. Common or great, none of us will ever be completely free of trouble. It's good to remember that not all of life's troubles are permanent. People tend to be happiest when they overcome difficulties and solve problems as they feel good about themselves.

Somehow adversity tends to stiffen our backbones and hardens our will. William Feather said, "Unless a man has been kicked around a little, you can't really depend on him to amount to much." JCPenney declared, "I would never have amounted to anything were it not for adversity. I was forced to come up the hard way." Yet for all our misfortunes, our troubles are ours alone. Socrates observed, "If all our misfortunes were laid in one common heap, whence everyone must take an equal portion, most people would be content to take their own and depart." So when our troubles seem overwhelming, we need to look around. We might find that things are not so bad after all.

Morris Goodman woke up on March 10, 1981, feeling good. He had it all, a loving wife, a beautiful home, a successful insurance business…and a new airplane. He decided to take a flight over Chesapeake Bay and as he was returning to the airstrip his engine failed and the plane hit power lines and crashed. He was injured so severely the doctors didn't think he would live through the night. X-rays revealed the two upper vertebrae in his neck were fractured and his spinal cord had been crushed leaving him paralyzed from the neck down. He was not able to breathe on his own or speak or swallow. He also sustained severe injuries to his liver, kidneys, larynx and diaphragm. All he could do was blink his eyes. Surgeons worked for nine hours to fuse his neck from the base of his head to the fourth cervical vertebrae, a surgery that had never been done before. After the surgery was completed, Morris and his wife were informed he would have to use a respirator for the rest of his life in order to breathe. He was also told he would never speak, eat, drink or walk again. The best hope was he would be able to sit in a wheelchair with a respirator. His sister noticed Morris could blink his eyes so she created charts which contained the alphabet and other symbols each correlating to a particular number. The number of blinks corresponded to a letter or object in the chart. This allowed Morris to communicate. Morris saw himself in his mind's eye, off the respirator and walking. He used visualization techniques and listened to Zig Ziglar and other motivational speakers on tape. Approximately two months after the accident, Morris was fitted with a halo vest. For weeks he tried to take a breath using his stomach muscles. Finally, he managed a couple of breaths and twelve weeks after the accident he was able to breathe on his own. A few weeks later, he was able to say his first word – mama. Morris continued to receive physical and occupational therapy. He walked out of the hospital on his own on November 13, 1981. After he was released from the hospital, Morris continued to receive therapy, including chiropractic. His positive experience with chiropractic inspired Morris to give a special presentation to chiropractors. I was privileged to be at the Parker Seminar in Dallas, Texas, when he spoke. Morris continues his life as a motivational speaker and author. He is known as "The Miracle Man."

It has been said life is 10% what happens to you and 90% how you react to it. It's important we hang in there and keep working to make things better. Chances are if we remain steadfast through our darkest times, we will eventually tap into some inner strength which will allow us to win in the end. You cannot have success without hardships and trials. Some folks quit and others take the punches and move on. They know their strength comes from struggle and they make stepping stones out of stumbling blocks.

Television and movie star Michael J. Fox has Parkinson's disease and still manages to work and stay enthusiastic about life. Parkinson's is an incurable disease which causes trembling, slowness and rigidity. The cause is unknown. Most people who end up with this disease feel the onset at about age 50. Michael was 30 when he noticed the first symptoms. Yet Michael continues to enjoy his work, years after doctors said he would be unable to continue. His resolve is firm and his attitude is remarkable. Michael said, "I wake up curious every day and every day I'm surprised by something. And if I can just recognize that surprise every day and say, 'Oh, that's a new thing, that's a new gift that I got today that I didn't even know about yesterday;' it keeps me going. It keeps me more than going. It keeps me enthusiastic and grateful." Michael said it keeps him "enthusiastic, curious and grateful." How wonderful is that? If anyone has the right to complain, it would be him…but here he is waking up curious and looking for the gifts of life. To me that says a lot about the man's character. Many times, character is developed through adversity. As Helen Keller pointed out, "Character cannot be developed in ease and quiet. Only through experience of trial and suffering can the soul be strengthened, vision cleared, ambition inspired, and success achieved." People who have overcome adversity were determined to grow from that experience. They say that hardship in life is what carbon is to steel. Cavet Roberts said, "We grow strong in the crucible of adversity." We are tested through hardships. Tough times in the past help us to prepare for greater things in the future.

Another person who overcame great adversity was Wilma Rudolph. She was born prematurely and weighed only 4 ½ pounds. At four years of age, she developed polio and had to wear a leg brace on her left leg for five years. She had to wear orthopedic shoes for the next two years and her doctors said she would never walk normally. But Wilma never gave up and eventually became a basketball star who set state records while in high school. At age 16, she earned a spot on the 1956 Olympic team and won a bronze medal in the 4 X 10 relay in Melbourne, Australia. At the Olympic games in Rome in 1960, she won three gold medals despite running on a sprained ankle. She was so graceful the Italian press called her the "Black Gazelle." When asked about her earlier struggles, Wilma said, "My doctor told me that I would never walk again but my mother said I would; I believed my mother."

Adversity helps to keep us humble and causes us to turn to God. It teaches us to turn our troubles over to a higher power. It seems real difficulties can be overcome; only the imaginary ones stop us dead in our tracks. When adversity comes it is helpful to remember that "this too shall pass." We need to accept the reality of the situation but not its permanence. Franklin D. Roosevelt had his share of troubles but gave us this advice, "When you reach the end of your rope, tie a knot and hang on."

Adversity helps us to dig deeper and try harder to overcome. It makes us stronger and increases our will power and resolve. Somehow it brings out the best in us. It changes our attitude in the way we look at what happens to us and develops virtues we may not have developed otherwise. Samuel Johnson summed it up so succinctly, "He knows not his own strength who hath not met adversity." It's important to learn from our setbacks as they can lead to different approaches to a problem or situation. Setbacks can ultimately lead to a comeback. We must pull ourselves up by our bootstraps, keep the faith and stay positive. We need to focus on our goals and keep trying. I like what Don King had to say about setbacks, "This is a setback. You get back up, you dust yourself off, and you get back in the game. We had a great singer named Ray Charles who wrote a song called "Drowning In My Tears." You can't afford to drown in your tears. You gotta go back, rededicate yourself, redouble your efforts and persevere."

"Adversity has the effect of eliciting talents, which in prosperous circumstances, would have lain dormant."
Horace

"When we long for life without difficulties, remind us that oaks grow strong in contrary winds and diamonds are made under pressure."
Peter Marshall

"Life is thickly sown with thorns, and I know no other remedy than to pass quickly through them. The longer we dwell on our misfortunes, the greater their power over us."
Voltaire

"No one could endure adversity, if while it continued, it kept the same violence that its first blows had…no state is so bitter that a calm mind cannot find in it some consolation. It is possible to soften what is hard…and burdens will press less heavily upon those who bear them skillfully."
Seneca

TAKEAWAY: ADVERSITY MAKES US STRONGER AND BRINGS OUT THE BEST IN US.

"All the art of living lies in a fine mingling of letting go and holding on."
-Havelock Ellis

"The hardest thing in life is to learn which bridge to cross and which to burn."
-David Russell

19

KNOW WHEN TO HOLD ON AND WHEN TO LET GO

One of the more challenging decisions we face in life is choosing to walk away or try harder. There is a huge difference between perseverance and knowing when you have had enough. It's usually best to persevere until you get your second wind but sometimes, in your heart, you know that it is useless. It's good to remember everyone has problems unless they are in a cemetery; problems are a part of life. If you are on the river of life, it's likely that you will hit a few rocks! Most problems have a limited lifespan. Some turn out to be benefits in the long run. Wayne Dyer said, "It takes great learning to understand that all things, events, encounters and circumstances are helpful."

Learning how to handle adversity is probably one of the most important things we can ever accomplish in life. Victory over challenges and obstacles enhance your quality of life as there is great joy and satisfaction in overcoming adversity. Cavett Robert said, "We grow strong in the crucible of adversity." Adversity sharpens us as it causes us to grow. Life's hurts will ever make you better or bitter. W. Clement Stone is credited with saying, "Every adversity has the seed of an equivalent or greater benefit." Adversity can defeat us or make us more determined. We need to keep adversity in perspective. There is an old saying that says, "When the night is blackest, the stars shine the brightest."

It is important that we learn to bounce back from disappointments and defeats quickly. If we attempt to accomplish a certain task and fail, it's okay because we did the best that we could. We can go on to accomplish other goals. I like what former undisputed heavyweight champion Joe Frazier said about the possibility of defeat, "If I lose, I'll walk away and never feel bad…because I did all I could; there was nothing more to do." In contrast, Harold Stassen, a former governor of Minnesota, ran for president ten times and was never elected or even nominated. It's important to realize when you no longer have a chance at winning. Cut your losses and go on to other things. Perhaps, Mr. Stassen could have been elected to the House of Representatives or the United States Senate as he had a great deal of talent.

"Let go or be dragged."
-Zen Proverb

"To reach a port we must sail, sometimes with the wind, and sometimes against it. But we must not drift or lie at anchor."
-Oliver Wendell Holmes

TAKEAWAY: IF YOU HAVE A SHOT KEEP GOING, BUT IF NOT, LET IT GO.

Dr. Myren D. Anderson

"The good life is begun at daybreak, formed at every wave, has your destiny prewritten on it."
—Ray Davis, Senior

"Do not dwell in the past, do not dream of the future. Concentrate the mind on the present moment." —Buddha

"You must live in the present, launch yourself on every wave, find your eternity in each moment."
-Henry David Thoreau

"Do not dwell in the past, do not dream of the future. Concentrate the mind on the present moment."-Buddha

20

PRESENT TIME CONSCIOUSNESS (PTC)

Life is composed of a succession of moments. It is important that we keep our mind centered on the here and now and not so much on the past or the future. William Somerset Maugham said, "The passing moment is all we can be sure of; it is only common sense to extract its utmost value from it." William Shakespeare wrote, "Like as the waves make towards the pebbled shore, so do our minutes hasten to their end." Live all the minutes, hours and days of your life, mindful of how brief life really is. So, live in the moment; enjoy the moment; savor the moment!

Besides enjoying life more, being in the present time helps us avoid fear and guilt. Fear is worry about the future and tends to immobilize us which leads to procrastination and increased stress. Cervantes wisely said, "One of the effects of fear is to disturb the senses and cause things to appear other than what they are." Fear tends to increase anxiety. Jesus said, "Do not be anxious about tomorrow, for tomorrow will be anxious for itself. Let the day's own troubles be sufficient for the day." Present Time Consciousness eliminates fear, worry and anxiety.

Worry is a troubled state of mind which causes anxiety and distress about future events which may or may not occur. Worry is a form of fear. Anyone who has a tendency to worry is encouraged to read the book, "How To Stop Worrying and Start Living," by Dale Carnegie. This book is a classic which offers practical advice to help conquer worry.

Guilt is a powerful emotion which has destroyed the lives of countless individuals. Guilt is a feeling that you have done something wrong. Guilt causes people to commit suicide, drink too much, to become depressed, etc. Guilt causes us to dwell on the past, reliving previous indiscretions and tends to lessen the joy of the present moment. We must forgive ourselves to get rid of guilt. Longfellow observed, "Look not mournfully into the past; it comes not back again. Wisely, improve the present; it is the thing. Go forth to meet the shadowy future without fear and a manly heart." We must learn from the past but live in the now. Always make today your best day. Will Rogers put it this way, "Don't let yesterday use up too much of today."

In 2013, Nik Wallenda, a member of the famous Flying Wallendas' circus family, made history when he walked across a portion of the Grand Canyon on a two-inch steel cable. Without a net or safety harness, Wallenda accomplished the feat by thanking God with each step and by utilizing visualization and concentration techniques. I believe it is fair to say Nik Wallenda has mastered the art of Present Time Consciousness (PTC). Another individual reported to be a master of PTC is former President Bill Clinton. It has been said that when he speaks to an individual it is though there isn't another person in the world as far as he is concerned. He is totally with and in tune with the person he is conversing with. They say you may forget what he said but you will never forget how he made you feel.

Present time consciousness means we live in the now, so our awareness is increased and we enjoy life more. Oliver Wendell Holmes Jr. used this example, "If you want to hit a bird on the wing you must have all your will in focus, you must not be thinking about yourself and, equally, you must not be thinking about your neighbor. You must be living in your eye on that bird on the wing." Life is short so it is important for us to learn to enjoy every moment of our lives as life is made up of moments. The present is a moment in time between the recent past and the near future. Moments may be temporary and fleeting but the memories can last a lifetime. People get into a rut and get so busy working that they forget about enjoying life. We need to take time to enjoy the beautiful sunrises and sunsets and to feel the breeze on your face when you're outside. Take the time to notice the shape of the clouds and the colors of things around you. We can be on automatic pilot so often we never really enjoy life. As Dr. Seuss said, "Sometimes you will never know the true value of a moment until it becomes a memory." The Roman poet, Horace, put it this way: "Carpe Diem" (seize the day). "Put no trust in the morrow." Live in the now. The past is over; the future is yet to be.

Look To This Day

Look to this day, for it is life-
the very life of life!
Within it lie all the verities
and realities of your existence:
the bliss of growth,
the glory of action,
the splendor of beauty.
For yesterday is only a dream
and tomorrow is only a vision;
but today well-lived
makes every yesterday
a dream of happiness
and every tomorrow
a vision of hope.
Look well, therefore, to this day!
Such is the salutation of the dawn.
from the Sanskrit

There are two days in every week about which we should not worry, two days which should be kept free from fear and apprehension.

One of these days is YESTERDAY with its mistakes and cares, its faults and blunders, its aches and pain. YESTERDAY is passed forever beyond our control.

All the money in the world cannot bring back YESTERDAY. We cannot undo a single act we performed; we cannot erase a single word we said. YESTERDAY IS GONE.

The other day we should not worry about is TOMORROW with it's possible adversities, it's burdens, its large promise and poor performance. TOMORROW is also beyond our immediate control.

TOMORROW'S sun will rise, either in splendor or behind a mask of clouds – but it will rise. Until it does, we have no stake in TOMORROW, for it is yet unborn.

This leaves only one day – TODAY. Any man can fight the battles of just one day. It is only when you and I add the burden of those two awful eternities – YESTERDAY and TOMORROW – that we break down.

It is not the experience of TODAY that drives men man – it is remorse or bitterness for something which happened YESTERDAY and the dread of what TOMORROW may bring.

"Let us therefore, live one day at a time." -Anonymous

"Life lived for tomorrow will always be just one day away from being realized."
Leo Buscaglia

"The art of life is to live in the present moment."
Emmet Fox

"If you are depressed, you are living in the past. If you are anxious, you are living in the future. If you are at peace, you are living in the present."
Lao Tzu

"For yesterday is but a dream
and tomorrow is only a vision
but today, well lived,
makes every yesterday
a dream of happiness
and every tomorrow a vision of hope."
Desiderata by Max Ehrmann

TAKEAWAY: EVERYDAY IS LIKE A NEW LIFE. LIVE IT WELL.

"The darkest day, lived till tomorrow, will have passed away." –William Cowper

"It takes great learning to understand that all things, events, encounters, and circumstances are helpful." –Wayne Dyer

21

ANTICIPATE THE GOOD EVEN DURING THE BAD

We all have some adversity or misfortune in greater or lesser degrees throughout our lives. It either breaks us or makes us stronger. William Arthur Ward said, "Adversity causes some men to break; others to break records." Setbacks and apparent defeats should be thought of as seminars that we took to learn the game of life. Setbacks can pave the way for greater comebacks. Consider the words of William James, "Be willing to have it so. Acceptance of what has happened is the first step in overcoming the consequences of any misfortune." The bad things in life open our eyes to all the good things we weren't paying attention to before. It is important to remember that down cycles are always followed by up cycles. The tide always comes back, and nothing lasts forever. Know that for every problem there is a solution or at least a limited time span. Meet life with an enthusiastic attitude and expectation of good. Always cling to hope as it provides relief from worry, anxiety, depression and discouragement. I love Orison Swett Marden's observation, "There is no medicine like hope, no incentive so great, and no tonic so powerful as expectation of something tomorrow." We need to press on and go forth with faith, anticipation, and expectancy. Pliny the Elder put it like this, "Hope is the pillar that holds up the world. Hope is the dream of the working man." Never lose hope; you never know what good tomorrow will bring.

You can fight hard times, or you can overcome hard times. Free your mind from worry and doubt and know that difficulties in life can make us better. We all have some hard times in life but we must not let ourselves believe that life is hard. Keep your thoughts on the present time. Think of why it will work and not why it won't. You must do things on faith alone. Know that everything will work out in your favor.

During down times, we must remember it is always darkest just before the dawn. Do not talk about your challenges and difficulties as what you talk about tends to come about. Consider the words of Voltaire who said, "Life is thickly sown with thorns, and I know no other remedy than to pass quickly through. The longer we dwell on our misfortunes, the greater is their power to harm us." During dark times, know that the tide is turning, and the dawn is coming. The tide of destiny will turn. Things will get better soon. If you see good in all things, the pump will be primed to bring more good things into your life. Keep adversity in perspective. If you suffer a setback and overcome it, you will be stronger because of it. Epictetus said, "It's not what happens to you, but how you react to it that matters." It has been said that things turn out best for people who make the best out of the way things turn out. Sophocles offered this advice, "There is no sense in crying over spilled milk. Why bewail what is done and cannot be recalled." When you hit turbulence, rise above it. Adversity has a way of building us up and teaches us the way we should go. As Norman E. Rosenthal, M.D. wrote, "The most valuable lessons came from difficult times – whether they were the result of bad luck, errors of judgment on my part, or self-imposed challenges. Adversity has made me more resilient and has helped me become a kinder, wiser, and better person."

I'll close this section with words from Williams Gaines, "Most of my major disappointments have turned out to be blessings in disguise. So, whenever anything bad happens to me, I kind of sit back and feel, well, if I give this enough time, it will turn out that this was good, so I shan't worry about it too much."

Dr. Myren D. Anderson

"When fate hands you a lemon, make lemonade."
-Dale Carnegie

"This, too, shall pass."
-William Shakespeare

"God will not permit any troubles to come upon us, unless he has a specific plan by which great blessings can come out of difficulty."
-Peter Marshall

TAKEAWAY: LOOK UP – LOOK OUT. TOMORROW WILL BE BETTER.

"Besides the noble art of getting things done, there is the noble art of leaving things undone. This wisdom of life consists in the elimination of non-essentials." -Lin Yutang

"A little simplification would be the first step toward rational living, I think." -Eleanor Roosevelt

22

THE POWER OF SIMPLICITY

Most people live a life of obligations and deadlines which causes stress. People spend their free time going to endless ballgames and meetings for school and work. Everyone is in a hurry to go somewhere to do something. It's time to reevaluate our priorities and get back to a simpler, less complicated and more enjoyable life.

Technology has not helped. Many people are hopelessly addicted to their electronic devices. Some folks cannot even eat a meal without texting or calling someone on their cell phone. Kids are so addicted to their electronic games that they neither hear nor see you when you try to communicate with them. Facebook activities consume priceless hours of some people's lives.

Advertising has become so effective that most people are overwhelmed and burdened with credit cards and other types of debt. Marketers have one goal and that is to make you discontent with what you have so you buy something you don't really need. The problem is that we have unlimited desires with a limited income. Keeping up with the Jones' is becoming ever more difficult. Sure the new boat or motor home is nice but now you have to pay for it with monthly installments for the next five or six years or more. You also have to pay interest, insurance and maintain it. Rather than purchasing a motorhome, for example, why not rent one? If you purchase one, you'll only use it a few times the first year and even less the following years. You can rent boats, motorcycles, snowmobiles and other recreational vehicles. It will make your life simpler with a lot less stress.

John Stuart Mill said, "I have learned to seek my happiness by limiting my desires, rather than in attempting to satisfy them." Perhaps, we need to appreciate what we already have. It is good to simplify our lives and to make them less complicated as the result will be greater happiness and satisfaction. "Simplicity is the ultimate sophistication", said Leonardo Da Vinci. I am not advocating that we sell our worldly goods and live in a self-built cabin in the woods, but I do feel we need to limit our desires. We also need to appreciate what we already have instead of striving for more things. The more things we have, the more complicated our lives become. Confucius said, "Life is really simple, but we insist on making it complicated. Learn to appreciate the little things in life as the big ones don't come around very often. Be content with what you have and realize that nothing is really lacking."

We need to slow down and enjoy life. It's time to turn off the gadgets and get on with actual living. Instead of texting endlessly, why not take a walk with a friend and have a real eyeball to eyeball conversation. Robert Louis Stevenson stated, "Talk is by far the most accessible of pleasures. It costs nothing in money, it is all profit, it completes our education, founds and fosters our friendships, and can be enjoyed at any age and in almost any state of health." How about a return to letter writing? The receiver can reread a letter several times increasing the enjoyment. The writer gets to enjoy putting thoughts to paper with the realization that he or she has brightened someone's life.

Enjoying nature and the natural world costs us nothing and rewards us with beauty, peace, relaxation, enjoyment and contentment. It lowers our blood pressure, enhances our senses, relaxes our muscles and reduces our cares. Nature helps us enjoy life to a greater extent. Dr. Larry Markson had this to say, "When you take time to commune with nature, you put balance and perspective back into your life." John Burroughs put it this way, "To find the universal elements enough; to find the air and water exhilarating; to be refreshed by a morning walk or an evening saunter…to be thrilled by the stars at night; to be elated over a bird's nest or a wildflower in the spring – these are some of the rewards of a simple life." God has created a universe filled with treasures. It is up to us to see the beauty in common simple things. Henry David Thoreau provided us with this insight, "That man is rich whose pleasures are the cheapest."

Fishing, hunting, hiking and camping are a few excellent ways of spending time to help rest the weary mind and body. Many people think the goal of the fisherman is to catch fish but what the person really wants is a change in scenery, some solitude and quiet time enjoying nature. I think Charles Dudley Warner said it well, "To poke a wood fire is more solid enjoyment than almost anything else in the world." So get out of the office and house and enjoy the tranquility, the solitude and the beauty of nature. Learn to see beauty in everyday common things. Take time to enjoy a spectacular sunrise or sunset. See the beauty in a flower. Notice the fragrances of the trees and flowers. Take a walk to see if you can see a deer or rabbit. Taking a walk with your dog can be one of your greatest joys. It's very relaxing and good for your heart health as well. Epictetus said it like this, "The essence in philosophy is that a man should so live that his happiness shall depend as little as possible on external things." We don't need things to be happy; we can do things to make us happy instead.

Hobbies are another great way to enjoy living simple. Knitting, crocheting, card playing, Sudoku, puzzles, gardening, coin and stamp collecting, sewing, quilting, painting and reading are all examples of hobbies which enhance our life with greater enjoyment. Activities of this nature help to keep our minds mentally fit, as well. Physical hobbies such as lawn work, gardening and golf tend to keep people physically fit. Be sure to set aside some free time for spontaneous and unexpected activities as well.

Meditation is another activity that enhances our lives and it helps to slow us down and unwind. Meditation can be done anytime during the day but some find it best to do it early in the morning or the last thing at night. Meditation helps us look inward so we learn about the inner "me." When we take the time to meditate, it tends to still the mind so universal intelligence can speak to us in the form of hunches and intuition.

It is important that we stay socially active but it is equally important we are not overwhelmed with activities which are unnecessary. You can be so busy trying to change the world that you do not have a life. Many of these activities are merely ego trips and you end up like a dog chasing its tail. Socrates said it beautifully, "Beware of the barrenness of a busy life." SIMPLIFY YOUR LIFE!

"Whoever does not regard what he has as most ample wealth, is unhappy, though he be master of the world."
Epictetus (Greek Philosopher)

"Simplicity, simplicity, simplicity! I say, let your affairs be as two or three, and not a hundred or a thousand…simplify, simplify."
Henry David Thoreau

"Manifest plainness, embrace simplicity, reduce selfishness, have few desires."
Lao Tzu

TAKEAWAY: GET RID OF THE "CLUTTER" IN YOUR LIFE. EXAMINE YOUR LIFE AND SEE HOW YOU CAN SIMPLIFY IT.

Dr. Myren D. Anderson

"If you start to take Vienna, take Vienna."
-Napoleon Bonaparte

"Either do not attempt at all, or go through with it."-Ovid

23

COMPLETE CYCLES

Many people start a project and work on it for a while but then lose interest and the project is not completed. This is an incomplete cycle. An uncompleted cycle holds our attention and acts like a monkey on your back as you keep thinking about it, wasting vital energy and feeling bad because you never completed what you started. If a task is not completed it creates guilt which is one of the most powerful emotions. Guilt is worry over the past. Many times our greatest weariness and fatigue comes from work which is undone. If a person starts several projects and doesn't finish them, their life will become confused, hurried and stressed. Incomplete cycles drain you and dissipate your energy, as well. Joe Namath once said, "If you aren't going all the way, why go at all." Scripture says, "Whatever thy hand findeth to do, do it with all thy might."- Eccl. 9:10. A completed cycle on the other hand, has a beginning and an end. You started a project and finished it and now you have a successful experience. A completed cycle frees up your mind. This results in an improved self-image, a greater sense of accomplishment and efficiency. You have a good feeling about yourself and this invigorates you. As you learn to complete cycles, you'll have more time in your life for more projects. You will be much more organized and efficient. Benjamin Franklin said it best, "Perform without fail what you resolve." Euripedes observed, "Do not plan for ventures before finishing what's at hand." Procrastination is closely related to not completing cycles. In this case, you can't get started and you postpone or delay taking actions on things that should be done now. Napoleon Hill summed it up best when he said, "Procrastination is the bad habit of putting off until the day after tomorrow what should have been done the day before yesterday." Our greatest fatigue and weariness comes from work which is not completed. So make a list of all incomplete cycles and complete them in order of their priority. This will free your mind and give you a greater sense of self-worth.

"What is not started today is never finished tomorrow."
-Johann Wolfgang von Goethe

"Nothing is so fatiguing as the eternal hanging on of an uncompleted task."
-William James

"Much of the stress that people feel doesn't come from having too much to do. It comes from not finishing what they've started."
- David Allen

TAKEAWAY: FINISH WHAT YOU START SO YOU GET IT OFF YOUR MIND.

Dr. Myren D. Anderson

"To him who is in fear everything rustles."
-Sophocles

"Worry never robs tomorrow of its sorrow, it only saps today of its joy."-Leo Buscaglia

"Guilt is to the spirit, what pain is to the body."
-David A. Bednar

24

THREE DEADLY EMOTIONS: FEAR, WORRY AND GUILT

Three of the most-deadly emotions are fear, worry and guilt. Buddha said, "All that we are is the result of our thinking." We have to be careful of what we think about because what we think about most often is what expands in our lives. It is up to us to choose peaceful, loving thoughts and to let go of our fears, worries and guilt.

F.E.A.R. (False Evidence Appearing Real) is a very dangerous emotion. It has probably immobilized and defeated more people than any other thing. Whatever we tend to fear becomes manifested in our lives. There are many fears: fear of failure, fear of success, fear of poverty, fear of loss, fear of sickness, fear of death, etc. It is important we do not give faith to our fears. We tend to defeat fear if we act but have more fear if we postpone action. Faith in God can help to alleviate our fears. The Bible says, "I will fear no evil for thou art with me." (Psalms 23:4) Dale Carnegie made this observation concerning fear: "You can conquer almost any fear if you will only make up your mind to do so. For remember, fear doesn't exist anywhere except in the mind." We should never let our fears grow bigger than our faith. It is important we learn to conquer fear because if we don't, fear will destroy our confidence and our life. It causes us to give up and not even try. It causes undue stress and tends to wear us down. Reverend Robert H. Schuller said, "If you listen to your fears, you will die never knowing what a great person you might have been." We must live our dreams and not our fears. Fear is a destructive emotion as it causes us to become immobilized. Thomas Carlyle put it like this, "The first duty of man is to conquer fear; he must get rid of it, he cannot act till then." Cervantes said,

"One of the effects of fear is to disturb the senses and cause things to appear other than what they are." Bertrand Russell said, "To conquer fear is the beginning of wisdom."

Worry is a state of mind which is closely related to fear. Worry is a misuse of your imagination which tends to run wild. You start to see things in your imagination that you do not want. You tend to act like your own self executioner as worry causes increased stress, tension, and anxiety. An unknown author said, "Worry is a complete cycle of inefficient thought revolving around a pivot of fear." Mahatma Gandhi observed, "There is nothing that wastes the body like worry, and one who has any faith in God should be ashamed to worry about anything." Worrying about the future takes the joy, happiness and health out of the present. Experts say that 95% of what we worry about never happens. Winston Churchill conveyed this message when he said, "I remember the story of the old man who said on his deathbed that he had a lot of trouble in his life most of which never happened." The antidote to worry is purposeful action as it is difficult to work and be worried at the same time. Thomas A. Edison humorously wrote, "As a cure for worrying, work is better than whiskey." Perhaps Napoleon Bonaparte had the best advice, "Throw off your worries as you throw off your clothes at night."

Guilt is a feeling of responsibility or remorse for some past action or offense which may be real or imagined. It is also a very powerful and destructive emotion. It's a heavy burden to carry and stops a person from enjoying life. When we feel guilty, we feel worthy of blame. Guilt causes resentment, ill health and depression. It also makes a person feel less deserving and tends to draw punishment to the individual. Forgiveness helps us get rid of our guilt, so we need to ask God for forgiveness. We also need to forgive ourselves for making a mistake. Foster Hibbard said saying "forgive me" frequently tends to dispel guilt. Forgiving yourself is just as important as forgiving others. Just as worrying can't change the future, no amount of guilt can change the past. Guilt is self-imposed anger for what we did or did not do. It is good to remember that a few mistakes do not define our life and we must not live in the past because of guilt. Choose to live in the present (present time consciousness). We also need to remember that this is your life. Don't let anyone make you feel guilty for living your life as you see fit.

"If you let your fear of consequences prevent you from following your deepest instinct, your life will be safe, expedient and thin."
-Katherine Butler Hathaway

"I release all feelings of worry and guilt. Throughout life, the two most futile emotions are guilt for what has been done and worry about what might be done."
-Wayne Dyer

"Guilt is the gift that keeps on giving."
-Erma Bombeck

"The purpose of guilt is to bring us to the Lord. After that it has no purpose."
-Mother Teresa

TAKEAWAY: FEAR, WORRY AND GUILT TAKE THE FUN OUT OF LIFE.

"Success is the maximum utilization of the ability that you have." -Zig Ziglar

"Success is going from failure to failure without loss of enthusiasm." -Winston Churchill

25

SUCCESS: LIVING YOUR LIFE AS YOU SEE FIT

Webster's New World Dictionary defines success as "a favorable or satisfactory outcome or result". Many folks measure success by the amount of power or wealth they attain; others consider themselves successful if they reach a certain station in life or achieve fame. Success is different for each individual as we all have our own priorities and goals in life. Each of us has unique programming so we see things differently. Earl Nightingale defined success as follows, "Success is the progressive realization of a worthy goal." Logan Pearsall Smith had this to say about success, "How can I say my life is not a success? Have I not for more than sixty years gotten enough to eat and escaped from being eaten?"

Making large amounts of money alone does not make one a success. An anonymous writer wrote the following: "Money will buy a bed, but not sleep; books, but not brains; food, but not appetite; finery, but not beauty; a house, but not a home; medicine, but not health; luxuries, but not culture; amusement, but not happiness; religion, but not spirituality." Bob Harrington, the chaplain of Bourbon Street said, "A person must be successful in all areas in life: physical, mental, spiritual, social, financial and family." We are not successful if you lose your soul or your family, for example. Aristotle, the famous ancient Greek philosopher wrote the following over 2,000 years ago, "All men seek one goal: success or happiness. The only way to achieve true success is to express yourself completely in service to society. First, have a definite, clear, practical ideal-a goal, an objective. Second, have the necessary means to achieve your ends-wisdom, money, materials and methods. Third, adjust all your means to that end." Ralph Waldo Emerson gave this opinion concerning success, "To laugh often and love much; to win the respect of intelligent people and affection of children; to earn the approbation of honest critics and endure the betrayal of false friends; to appreciate beauty; to find the best in others; to give oneself; to leave the world a bit better, whether by a healthy child, a garden patch, or a redeemed social condition; to have played and laughed with enthusiasm and sung with exaltation; to know even one life has breathed easier because you have lived-this is to have succeeded."

In order to be successful and to enjoy success, we must live a life of purpose. It's not enough to go to work. We need to go to work because it's our life. Our work should be our passion and should satisfy our desire to accomplish something and to be respected. Our work needs to satisfy our need to be relevant and to be needed. You are not just laying bricks, you are building a cathedral, for example. If you love your work, you'll never work a day in your life as your purpose is larger than just earning a paycheck. George Burns had this to say, "Fall in love with what you are going to do for a living. To be able to get out of bed and do what you love to do for the rest of the day is beyond words. I'd rather be a failure in something I love than be successful in something I hate." If you love your work, you get into flow and time really flies. You feel good and you do good work. Successful people look at their work in terms of the privilege it gives them to grow as a person.

Risk taking is an important quality that most successful people have learned to develop. You must expand your comfort zone and do the things less successful people wouldn't even attempt. Winston Churchill put it this way, "Only those who have dared to fail greatly can ever achieve greatly." We need to think outside the box and to try new things in a different way. Unless you are willing to take a chance, you'll never get the reward. Dreams never become a reality without some risk. If you want different results in your life, you must make different choices and that requires taking risks. There is no way to succeed without exposing yourself to risk. Being willing to fail greatly increases your ability to succeed as you are more likely to try different and more effective ways to accomplish your goal. The greatest risk is to be cautious and never attempt anything. Contrast that with the Apollo astronauts, Neil Armstrong and Buzz Aldrin who risked their lives to be the first humans to walk on the moon on July 21, 1969. There was no guarantee they would get to the moon and return to the Earth alive.

One of the major obstacles to success is inertia. Sometimes people get into a rut and drift. Nothing in the universe stands still. We are either going forwards or backwards. To overcome inertia, we need to take action steps. Do step one even if you don't know step two. Commit yourself to action and find the solution to problems as you go along. We must take the position that if it is to be, it is up to me. Nobody else can do it for us. It's not so much where we are now but in which direction we are heading. When opportunity knocks, we have to get up and answer. Don't wait until everything is "just right" because things are never exactly like we would like to have them. Thought determines what you want; action determines what you get. Never put off until tomorrow what you can do today. Do not procrastinate; take action now. There is an old saying, "Success is a ladder that you can't climb with your hands in your pockets." Vince Lombardi gave this assessment, "The price of success is hard work, dedication to the job at hand, and the determination that whether we win or lose, we have applied the best of ourselves to the task at hand."

Being ready when opportunities appear is essential for successful achievement. In order to be ready, we have to improve ourselves in several areas. We need to improve our knowledge about our work to the point that we become an expert. We need to work on our people skills, our attitude, and our communication skills. We also need to know exactly what we want. Most people spend more time deciding which car to buy rather than thinking about their life's work. Many take the first job offered and stay until retirement. William Mathews said, "The first law of success…is concentration: to bend all the energies to one point, and to go directly to that point, looking neither to the right nor the left."

Success in any endeavor is unlikely without a great amount of discipline. Discipline is the cornerstone of all achievement as it helps one to make short term sacrifices in order to achieve long term gain. Personal discipline takes you from your goals to actual achievements. Bob Richards, the great American Olympic athlete said, "One of the great lessons I've learned in athletics is that you've got to discipline your life. No matter how good you may be, you've got to be willing to cut out of your life those things that keep you from going to the top. "Each person must decide what he or she wants to accomplish in life and what they're willing to sacrifice to achieve it. Success means different things to each of us so we must define success according to our priorities. I believe Christopher Morley said it best, "There is but one success-to be able to spend your life in your own way."

"Your rewards in life are in direct ratio to your contribution, your service."
-Earl Nightingale

"Flaming enthusiasm, backed up by horse sense and persistence, is the quality that most frequently makes for success."
-Dale Carnegie

"I know the price of success: dedication, hard work and an unremitting devotion to things you want to see happen."
-Frank Lloyd Wright

TAKEAWAY: EACH PERSON DEFINES SUCCESS FOR HIMSELF

Dr. Myren D. Anderson

"I murmured because I had no shoes, until I met a man who had no feet." -Persian Proverb

"A thankful heart is not only the greatest virtue, but the parent of all other virtues."
 -Cicero

26

COUNT YOUR BLESSINGS

Webster's New World Dictionary defines gratitude as "a feeling of thankful appreciation for favors or benefits received". If we fill our hearts with gratitude you won't focus on what is missing. Giving thanks can actually change our lives and improve our well-being.

First and foremost, we need to be thankful for being alive. Life is good. It is such a privilege to be alive, but it is even better when we are healthy to really appreciate the wonderful world in which we live. I love Ralph Waldo Emerson's observation, "When I first open my eyes upon the morning meadows and look out upon the beautiful world, I thank God I am alive."

When we take the time to count our blessings and develop an attitude of gratitude, we tend to find more things to be grateful for. It is important to realize that God is a source of all blessings. Everything we have has been given to us by God. Everyone who has been a blessing to us has been influenced by God. Wallace D. Wattles said, "Gratitude draws the mind into closer touch with the source from which the blessings come."

We need to be grateful for food, clean water, clean air, good health, a roof over our heads, our family, our friends, the opportunity to work and play, peace, etc. We need to thank God each day for living in a country in which we are free to live, worship and work in the pursuit of happiness. The more we appreciate our blessings, the more our physical, mental, and spiritual health improves. Charles Dickens wrote, "Reflect upon your present blessings of which every man has many; not on your past misfortunes, of which all men have some." We need to remind ourselves frequently that our cup is really half full rather than half empty. Know that you are unbelievably blessed. For example: chances are you had at least two good meals today. Reflect on the fact that 30,000 people die of starvation somewhere in the world each day.

A friend of ours, in her 80s, was diabetic and in a nursing home. The doctors first amputated one leg and then the other. People who visited her were astonished as she spoke only of good things and good times. When someone mentioned her lost limbs she always said, "I still have my hands."

Thank God for every small thing or benefit that comes to you. Appreciate how far you have already come on the journey of life. Of all people of all ages, none have more reason for thanksgiving than you and I. Epicurus observed, "Do not spoil what you have by desiring what you have not; remember, that which you now have was once among the things only hoped for." Henri-Frederic Amiel said, "Thankfulness is the beginning of gratitude. Gratitude is the completion of thankfulness. Thankfulness may consist merely of words. Gratitude is shown in acts."

It is helpful to write down the things we are grateful for in a gratitude journal (a wins book) on a daily basis. We should do this as a discipline to keep us aware of our daily good. We tend to attract what we dwell on so we will attract more good when we acknowledge the good we've already received. I like what Dr. James W. Parker said about gratitude, "I will count my blessings and keep my mind on something going right." During up cycles we should show gratitude; during down cycles we should demonstrate patience. Seeing good in all things primes the pump to bring more good things into our lives. We should live with a grateful heart one day at a time. Savor small favors and gifts, as well as the large ones. Get excited about being alive and the ability to get out of bed in the morning. It could be over tomorrow. Give thanks to God for all things everyday. Refuse to have a "bad" day. Cavett Robert said, "If you don't think everyday is a good day, just try missing one." As John Milton wrote, "Gratitude bestows reverence, allowing us to encounter everyday epiphanies, those transcendent moments of awe that change forever how we experience life and the world." As Zig Ziglar reminds us, "Gratitude is the healthiest of all human emotions. The more you express gratitude for what you have, the more likely you will have even more to express gratitude for."

We should also express gratitude for what doesn't happen to us as well. An anonymous person once wrote, "If you can't be grateful for what you receive, be thankful for what you escape." Perhaps you avoided catching the flu…or getting killed in a car accident. Mathew Henry declared the following after being robbed, "I thank thee first because I was never robbed before; second, because although they took my purse, they did not take my life; third, because although they took my all, it was not much; and fourth, because it was I who was robbed, and not I who robbed." Perhaps, we should be grateful that God doesn't give us all the things that we ask for. If we got everything we asked for we would undoubtedly get ourselves into a lot of trouble and heartache. I believe we are given what we can handle. Focus on what you have no matter how insignificant. Praise and give thanks for the gifts in life that you receive. Don't take your good for granted.

Eddie Rickenbacker was an American fighter pilot in World War I and Medal of Honor recipient. He became an ace for 26 confirmed kills. In October of 1942, Rickenbacker was a passenger in a B-17B Flying Fortress on a mission to deliver a message from the president to General MacArthur in Port Moresby, New Guinea. The plane had to ditch in the ocean due to navigation error and Eddie and the crew of seven spent 27 days in life rafts in the Pacific Ocean. For two days they had no water or food. On the third day, they managed to collect rainwater from their clothes. They prayed and a few days later, a seagull landed on Rickenbacker's head and he caught it. The bird was divided among the crew, and they used the intestines as bait as they had fishing line and a couple of hooks in their survival gear. They caught enough fish to sustain them. During their time at sea, they fought off sharks that would ram their rafts. Eventually they were rescued by the Navy. Rickenbacker lost over 50 pounds during the ordeal. He was forever grateful to God for having answered their prayers and every Friday night until his death he fed the seagulls shrimp in appreciation and gratitude.

I came across this wonderful message while researching for this book. I include it here as a reminder that we must count our blessings each and every day.

EVERYDAY THANKSGIVING
Even though I touch my blanket and growl
when the alarm rings each morning,
    Thank you, Lord, that I can hear.
    There are those who are deaf.
Even though I keep my eyes tightly closed
against the morning lights as long as possible,
    Thank you, Lord, that I can see.
    There are many who are blind.
Even though I huddle in my bed and put off the
physical effort of rising,
    Thank you, Lord, that I have the strength to rise.
    There are many who are bedfast.
Even though the first hour of my day is hectic,
when socks are lost, toast is burned, tempers are short,
    Thank you, Lord, for my family.
    There are many who are lonely.
Even though our breakfast table never looks like the pictures
in the ladies' magazines, and the menu is at times unbalanced,
    Thank you, Lord, for the food we have.
    There are many who are hungry.
Even though the routine of my job is often monotonous,
    Thank you, Lord, for the opportunity to work.
    There are many who have no work.
Even though I grumble and bemoan my fate from day to day,
and wish my modest circumstances were not quite so modest,
    Thank you, Lord, for the gift of life. -Author Unknown

Count your blessing not your crosses,
Count your gains, not your losses.
Count your joys instead of your woes,
Count your friends instead of your foes.
Count your health, not your wealth.
Old Proverb

"What a wonderful life I've had! I only wish I'd realized it sooner."
-Colette

"He who is not contented with what he has, would not be contented with what he would like to have."
-Socrates

"I am grateful for what I am and have. My thanksgiving is perpetual."
-Henry David Thoreau

"God has given us a world that nothing but our folly keeps us from being a paradise."
-George Bernard Shaw

TAKEAWAY: GOD IS THE SOURCE OF ALL BLESSINGS.

"A man too busy to take care of his health is like a mechanic too busy to take care of his tools."
-Spanish Proverb

"It is health that is real wealth and not pieces of silver and gold."-Mahatma Gandhi

27

YOU ARE NEVER WEALTHY UNLESS YOU ARE HEALTHY

There are many blessings of life: friendship, happiness, peace of mind, contentment, food and shelter, success and good health. Money can buy a lot of things in this world, but it cannot buy health, the greatest of all blessings. I am reminded of the old Arabian Proverb which states, "He who has health has hope, and he who has hope has everything." It is important that we love ourselves enough to live a healthy lifestyle.

In 1948, the founders of the World Health Organization (WHO) defined health as "Physical, mental and social well-being, not merely the absence of disease." It is also the balance of mind, body and soul. When we get something for nothing, we tend to take it for granted. Most often we are born healthy and for many years our health is not really a concern. It is not until years later when the first symptoms appear that we even think about our health and even then, we tend to put off any efforts of self-help or even medical help. The following poem by an anonymous writer illustrates the point:

Dear Doctor:
I burn my candle at both ends,
don't tell me to relax- - - - - - -
just write me a prescription for
a longer burning wax.

ALWAYS CONSIDER YOURSELF HEALTHY

Visualize yourself in good health. Thinking makes it so. Constructive, healthful thoughts will produce health; whereas continued negative thoughts will produce disease. Our subconscious mind will produce in our bodies whatever we tell it to. If we continually think about cancer, heart trouble or how much trouble we have sleeping, we will get cancer, heart trouble or insomnia. If we think of health, we will do healthful things (exercise, watch diet, think positive, etc.) and the end result will be health. Be thankful for the health you have. Anticipate the good even when things may be going bad. Count your blessings! Even with the disabilities we may have, it is not hard to find someone who is worse off than we are. If you are already aged, consider yourself lucky for having lived so long.

List 25 health assets that you have at the present time. Review the list every week and you will soon be adding new reasons for which to be thankful. Mentally imagine yourself as being completely healthy. Constantly affirm: "I am healthy, I am strong. I am still young." Re-educate your mind so it accepts and therefore produces health.

You can be as healthy as you want to be if you are willing to do what is necessary to produce and maintain health. As Harry Gaze said, "Of course you have to die, but you don't have to die sick."

****

You attract into your life what you see in your mind's eye. So "see" yourself healthier and then act healthier (act as if). Bless your body. Praise your body. Appreciate your body. Give thanks for your health.

THOUGHTS CAN AFFECT YOUR HEALTH

According to the latest research, 75-90% of the patients a doctor sees have problems which are due at least in part to emotional disorders. Emotions of worry, fear, hate, anxiety, irritation, frustration, resentment, envy, and despair, are all important contributors of disease. Many researchers feel in the back of every illness or disease is a disordered state of mind. If your mind can make you sick through wrong thinking, it can make you well by thinking correctly. Therefore, the first step to the attainment of health is to eliminate negative thoughts and feelings. Thoughts such as "I'm tired," "I can't take it anymore," "What's the use?" "That gives me a pain," "I'm getting old," "That burns me up," "I've got a bad back," "I can't stand so and so," orders our subconscious mind to produce pain, ill health, misery, and premature old age. There is no limit to our capacity for making ourselves sick. Even complaining about the weather or the government affects your health. You must control your thinking. It can be directed in any direction you desire. Say to yourself, "I'm going to keep my thinking positive and my attitude will be calm and cheerful right now". The second step is to learn to think and feel in a positive, healthy manner.

DON'T TALK ABOUT IT

If you have pain, dizziness, cramps, etc., don't talk about it. First of all, it is burdensome and boring to others. Second, it adds re-enforcement to your subconscious mind to continue the disease process and third, children have big ears. A mother with menstrual cramps will most likely have a daughter with the same problem. Parents who are chronic bellyachers can give children the idea their bodies are hell-holes of aches, pains and disease. The family unit is often the number one cause of disease as the personality of a child is primarily molded in the home. The first five years are extremely important in the emotional development of a child.

Never dramatize your problems. Wayne Dyer said, "The less you verbalize, the less you will have to complain about." Think and talk only about good health, vitality and longevity. Remember your attitude towards health determines how much you will have. The only person you should talk to about your symptoms is your doctor. We must realize that health is a journey---not a destination. We have a great influence on our health by our lifestyle and the habits we have. Deepak Chopra said: "The way you think, the way you behave, the way you eat, can influence your life by 30 to 50 years." Our lifespan is determined by our lifestyle. Our body chemistry can be changed by our thoughts. Caroline Leaf, PhD said, "If you don't think properly your brain becomes toxic. The concept 'I am sick,' must be changed to 'I am healthy.' If you repeatedly say, 'I am sick or I don't feel well,' your subconscious mind will take you at your word and will see to it that you become sicker."

When one thinks of healing methods, medicine obviously comes to mind. Other methods include osteopathy, chiropractic, acupuncture, naturopathy, mind science, Chinese herbal medicine, etc. Any method which causes a patient to move from fear and worry to faith and expectancy will heal. Our bodies have an innate or inborn ability to heal. Nature is the greatest healer of all. The power that made the body can heal the body. It's been said "The surgeon makes the incision but God heals the body." The greatest doctor is inside the skin. William Osler said, "The good physician treats the disease; the great physician treats the patient who has the disease." Hippocrates, the father of medicine, said, "Natural forces within us are the true healers of disease." He also said, "To do nothing is sometimes a good remedy." More recently, Robert C. Peale, MD, said, "The best and most efficient pharmacy is within your own system." It's important to remind ourselves that all healing comes from God. As the scriptures remind us, "I will restore health unto thee, and I will heal thee of thy wounds, saith thy Lord…" Jeremiah 30:17

Albert Schweitzer, MD, put it this way, "Every patient carries his own doctor inside of him. We are at our best when we give the doctor who resides within each patient a chance to work." Bernie Siegal, MD, said, "My job as a physician is not only to find the right treatment but to help the patient find an inner reason for living, resolve conflicts, and free healing energy."

It's important we don't take too many medications. Several billion dollars a year is spent by drug companies to advertise drugs which in many cases only treat symptoms. You can't even watch the evening news without seeing several drug ads. The drug companies have one goal and that is to have every earthling from the basket to the casket on drugs. Talk to your doctor and see if you can get off medications which are not vital to your health and well-being. Medications can heal---or they can make you sick or even cause death. Sidney J. Harris said, "Most drugs that are strong enough to help you are also strong enough to hurt you, and there is no way out of that dilemma." William Osler said, "The desire to take medicine is perhaps the greatest feature which distinguishes man from animals." Americans consume 75% of the world's prescription drugs, yet we are just 5% of the world's population. The average 60-year-old patient takes about six prescription medications daily. Besides that, most people self-medicate with over the counter drugs. Many over-the-counter drugs actually prolong the misery. Let the body's natural defense mechanisms fight the disease without interference. It knows what it's doing.

The importance of adequate physical exercise cannot be over emphasized. Exercise is essential for the maintenance of health as it increases spinal mobility, increases blood flow to the brain and body, increases stamina, energy, and metabolism to help keep your weight down. It also improves sleep, reduces stress, keeps bones strong, helps to alleviate pain and improves the bodies, immune function. Man is about the only one of God's creatures that is too lazy to exercise. All other beings exercise regularly to keep their bodies fit. Stretching is common in the animal kingdom. Cats are doing a lot more than sharpening their claws when they tear up your curtains or davenport. They are, in fact, mobilizing their spine and stretching muscle groups. If an animal, such as a horse or cow is released from a prolonged period in the barn, the first thing they do is kick their legs in the air, run, jump and play. They are doing what their natural instincts tell them to do. Walking, swimming, stretching and deep breathing are just a few good exercises you can do. It is generally agreed by experts that we should walk about five miles a day. You are never too old to exercise, in fact, the older you get the more you need exercise. Your body was made to be used – so use it. It is much better to wear out than to rust out. There are many types of exercise. Aerobic exercises consist of cycling, swimming, biking, walking and using a treadmill. It also includes running at a slower pace. This type of exercise improves overall health and quality of life, burns fat, improves mood and improves cardiovascular health and endurance. Anaerobic exercise consists of weight lifting, sprinting and other high intensity activities. This type of activity helps to build lean muscle mass and to improve muscle strength and overall fitness and endurance. Flexibility exercises include stretching, yoga, Pilates etc. Balance training is especially important as we get older. A good method is to stand on one leg with eyes closed. A chair can be used for safety. Kenneth H. Cooper said, "The reason I exercise is for the quality of life I enjoy." Because man walks on two legs, gravity is one of our greatest challenges as the spine is under immense stress and is involved to some degree in practically every disease of mankind. Paul Bragg said, "You are only as old as your spine." Dr. Roger Sperry, Nobel Peace Prize recipient for brain research said, "Ninety percent of the stimulation and nutrition to the brain is generated by the movement of the spine. This would be analogous to a windmill generating electricity." It is vitally important that we take time for our health every day by exercising so that we have health for our time tomorrow. It has been said that an exercise a day gives you five more years to play. Health is our most precious gift. Not only will exercise keep our physical body healthy, but it will also help to keep us mentally sharp. President John F. Kennedy put it this way, "Physical fitness is not only one of the most important keys to a healthy body, it is the basis of dynamic and creative intellectual activity." Exercise improves the quality of our lives as it increases the level of endorphins in our bodies. Endorphins give you a positive reaction to life. Thomas Jefferson had this advice, "Exercise and application produces order in our affairs, health of body, cheerfulness of mind, and these make us precious to our friends."

Prevention is key in maintaining our health. Each of us must take an active interest in our healthcare. If we don't smoke, we can help prevent lung cancer and other diseases. If we keep our weight within reasonable levels, we can help prevent diabetes. Brushing our teeth can help prevent cavities, as another example. We must be proactive when it comes to our health. We can't just muddle along and hope for the best. One old timer said, "Gee Doc, if I'd have known I was going to live so long I'd have taken better care of myself." One of the problems with healthcare in the United States is that we've been conditioned to treat symptoms rather than preventing disease in the first place. Symptoms are like a red light on your car. It is a warning, telling you that something is wrong. Symptoms are the last to come and the first to go away. Just because you don't have symptoms doesn't mean you are healthy. Senator Tom Harkin summed it up when he said, "The American healthcare system is in crisis precisely because we symptomatically neglect wellness and prevention." Harvard Professor Rifat Atun makes a similar observation, "Don't wait for illness, invest in the maintenance of health… there needs to be an emphasis on maintaining good health, preventing disease, and slowing progression of disease when it does happen. There's no choice; it has to happen." To be healthy, a person needs to have adequate rest. This includes sleeping for 7 to 8 hours a night. Caffeine must be minimized or eliminated as it affects sleep. There needs to be a balance between work and rest, as well. Most people live an over-extended life as they are always in a hurry and are stressed. They are too busy to have a life. The great majority of people don't even know their neighbors and have never visited with them. Many don't even spend quality time with their spouse or children. Gerald Brenan said, "We are closer to the ants than to the butterflies. Very few people can endure much leisure." George Eastman put it this way, "What we do during our working hours determines what we have; what we do in our leisure hours determines what we are." People need to take vacations and have time enough to read a book, take a nap, listen to music or to go fishing. Having and enjoying leisure time is health producing. Logan Pearsall Smith reminds us, "If you are losing your leisure, look out, you may be losing your soul." There is great healing in the enjoyment of nature. There is something in the sound of the surf, the rhythmic sounds of a rain and the sound of leaves rustling in the woods that soothe a person's nerves. Even the absence of sound while in the woods is remarkable. Be sure to give yourself the gift of nature often. John Burroughs said, "I go to nature to be soothed and healed, and to have my senses put in order." John Muir put it this way, "Keep close to nature's heart…and break clear away, once in a while, and climb a mountain or spend a week in the woods. Wash your spirit clean." Nature takes you from pissed to bliss.

Don't smoke, as smoking ages you prematurely and may eventually cause lung cancer, heart trouble and death. Some doctors feel that smoking takes ten years off your life. If you smoke, stop, and if you haven't started, don't start. On a humorous note, they say kissing someone who smokes is a little like licking an ashtray! Chewing tobacco is also dangerous to your health and is a disgusting habit. Vaping isn't healthy either. Quit the tobacco habit entirely. Your life urges must be stronger than your death urges.

Minimize alcohol intake, as alcohol abuse causes cancer, heart disease, depression and also depresses the immune system. Alcohol is very addictive, and withdrawal can be extremely difficult. Avoid recreational drug use. I can't imagine any rational or sane person taking amphetamines, ecstasy, marijuana, LSD, cocaine, heroin or any other recreational drugs. Users must live a pathetic life.

Americans are perhaps the only people on earth who die prematurely because we eat too much. It has been said that your waistline determines your life span. Benjamin Franklin said, "Eat few suppers, and you'll need few medicines." He also said, "To lengthen thy life, lessen thy meals." We need to eat sensibly and slowly and to leave the table just a little hungry. We need to eat to live…and not to live to eat. Food should be considered fuel for our body and not as a salve to reduce boredom or to feel good. It's been said we should eat like a king for breakfast, a prince for lunch and a pauper for supper. Our meals need to be nutritionally balanced as well. It's helpful to fortify our diet with natural vitamins and mineral supplements, especially if you are growing, pregnant, elderly or are on prescription medications. Probiotics and whole food supplements are also helpful. It is essential we drink eight glasses of water daily and increase our fiber intake. Refrain from eating worthless foods such as chips and other snacks which are high in sugar or salt. In general, we should eat less red meat and more fish and poultry. It's good to eat more fruits and vegetables and less prepared foods which are highly processed and full of chemical additives. It's good to use healthy oils such as olive oil rather than hydrogenated oils which are used in many prepared and packaged foods. It is good to limit carbohydrates and to eat whole grain foods whenever possible. Sugar and salt intake should be reduced, and artificial sweeteners should be avoided, as well. Soft drinks should be limited to three a week. These measures will help to prevent obesity as well.

No sensible person would ride a roller coaster or other high-speed ride without being buckled in, yet they may think nothing of driving or riding in a car without using a seat belt. Statistics show fatalities involving non-belted occupants have been recorded as low as 12 mph. Your chance of being killed is almost 25 times greater if thrown from the car as your body can be thrown 150 feet. Three out of four crashes causing death occur within 25 miles of home. Don't get careless; use your seat belts.

People who have pets are generally healthier than those who do not. Dogs and cats are wonderful stress relievers and companions. People with pets also live longer, as well. It is an established fact that your lifestyle determines your life span. We must love ourselves enough to live a healthy lifestyle. Andrew Weil, MD, said, "Most disease is lifestyle related and preventable." Health comes to those who become health conscious and do the things that create optimum health and well-being. After all, the body we have is the only one we'll have to live in for the rest of our life. Bless your body, praise your body, appreciate your body and give thanks for your body. A person will only want to live as long as he or she feels good. There is an old saying that goes, "Father time is catching up with mother nature," and this is true for all of us to a greater or lesser degree. So, take time for your health as it's a precious gift that we tend to take for granted and don't really appreciate until you've lost it.

Adequate sleep is essential for health. Most people need 7 to 8 hours a night, but some can get along with less. Good rest allows the body to heal and refresh. Avoid coffee and other caffeinated drinks several hours before bedtime. It is not a good idea for people to read or watch TV in the bedroom. Bedrooms should only be used for sex and sleep. If you have trouble sleeping, get outside and do some physical work so you are tired when night comes. It's helpful to open the windows and let some fresh air in, weather permitting. Another helpful tip is to read 3 to 4 pages of the Book of Psalms just before bedtime.

Maintaining good health also requires that we use good judgment regarding sexual activity. Gonorrhea, chlamydia and syphilis infections are at an all-time high in the United States and in many parts of the world. A return to morality is certainly warranted. In fact, practically all of the problems of the world could be prevented by following the Ten Commandments.

>The only exercise some folks get is:
>Jumping to conclusions
>Flying off the handle
>Carrying things too far
>Dodging responsibility
>Pushing their luck
>-James N. Miller

"A merry heart doeth good like a medicine'"
-King Solomon

"The art of medicine consists of three things: the disease, the patient and the physician."
-Hippocrates

TAKEAWAY: OUR GREATEST WEALTH IS HEALTH

It's surprising how many persons go through life without ever recognizing that their feelings toward other people are largely determined by their feelings towards themselves, and if you're not comfortable within yourself you can't be comfortable with others."
-Sidney J. Harris

"If you aren't good at loving yourself, you will have a difficult time loving anyone, since you resent the time and energy you give another person that you aren't even giving to yourself."
-Barbara DeAngelis

28

YOU CAN'T LOVE ANOTHER UNTIL YOU LEARN TO LOVE YOURSELF

Webster's Dictionary defines love as "a strong affection for or attachment or devotion to a person or persons." It is a feeling of acceptance, caring and genuine warmth for another. Love means you are tolerant of another person's omissions, failures and faults. Love makes no demands and has no expectations. Love is seeing good (God) in another or yourself. Loving yourself and others makes one feel good. William Shakespeare said, "Love comforteth like sunshine after a rain." It is interesting to note that love is located between like and lust in the dictionary.

They say that you can't give love; you can only be loving. We need to be loving in all areas of our life. Dr. James W. Parker called this "The Love Concept." He said, "Practice the love concept; it develops a non-critical attitude toward yourself and others. See God in yourself and in others. Love everyone as a father, mother, brother, sister and child."

Love keeps no records of wrongs. Love is looking for good in others and ourselves. We need to accept people as they are and love them unconditionally. As Mother Teresa said, "If you judge people, you have no time to love them." We all make mistakes as each of us has some dysfunctional programming. It is helpful to recall what Dale Carnegie said about people, "When dealing with people, remember you are not dealing with creatures of logic, but creatures of emotion."

It is vitally important to love others but, it is even more important to love ourselves. It may be that all love starts with self-love. Jesus said, "Love your neighbor as you love yourself." You will solve many "people problems" by working on self-love as this leads to self-worth and when you see yourself as good, others will seem good in your eyes, as well. We must depend on ourselves for approval and a sense of self-worth. Forgive yourself for what you have done or not done. When we can accept our own imperfections, we can be more tolerant of others and their flaws and actions. It's good to adopt the attitude of Dennis Waitley who said, "Accept yourself as you are right now; an imperfect, changing, growing and worthy person." Leo Tolstoy put it this way, "If you look for perfection, you will never be content."

It is important that you treat yourself right. Love yourself enough to realize you deserve the best. Be patient with yourself and learn to forgive yourself. You need to be your own best friend. Do not seek approval from others; loving yourself is the only approval that works. Norman Vincent Peale observed, "It is of practical value to learn to like yourself. Since you must spend so much time with yourself you might as well get some satisfaction out of the relationship." So, work on self-love. You are the person you spend every waking moment with and the relationship you have with yourself sets the tone for every other relationship you will ever have. You can't develop compassion for others unless you develop compassion for yourself.

"I am somebody.
I am me.
I like being me.
And I need nobody to make me somebody."
-Louis L'Amour

"You yourself, as much as anybody in the entire universe, deserve your love and attention."
Buddha

"Accept everything about yourself-I mean everything. You are you and that is the beginning and the end-no apologies, no regrets."
Henry Kissinger

TAKEAWAY: LOVE YOURSELF SO YOU CAN LOVE OTHERS.

"Happiness is not a station you arrive at, but a manner of traveling."-Margaret Lee Runbeck (American Author 1905-1956)

"You cannot prevent the birds of sadness from passing over your head, but you can prevent them from making nests in your hair."-Confucius

29

HAPPINESS IS A JOURNEY…NOT A DESTINATION

Webster's New World Dictionary defines happiness as, "good fortune, luck, pleasure, joy and contentment." It is a feeling of great pleasure and satisfaction. Happiness is different for each of us, and we will all define it in different ways. Happiness is not achieved by great wealth or power. As Abd-Al-Rahnan, a powerful ruler said, "I have reigned above fifty years in victory or peace, beloved by my subjects, dreaded by my enemies, respected by my allies. Riches and honors, power, and pleasure, have awaited my call, nor does any earthly blessings seem to have been wanting…I have diligently numbered the days of pure and genuine happiness that have fallen into my lot. They amount to fourteen." Some of the richest and powerful people of the world are unhappy, depressed, and unfulfilled. We know that power and wealth do not guarantee happiness. Possessions do not bring happiness either.

It seems to me that people who are unhappy are those who think only of themselves. They tend to be quick to judge others and frequently hold grudges. They always tend to look at life in the most negative terms and look at their glass as being half empty rather than half full. They are ungrateful for the blessings of life. They tend to do the same things over and over yet expect different results. Many unhappy people do not work, and they don't play a lot either. They have few social and creative outlets. They sometimes take advantage of their fellow man as they are takers rather than givers. To be happy a person has to forget themselves and think of others.

Another reason for unhappiness is that people have a tendency to compare themselves and their circumstances with others-especially those who are doing better. It has been said that comparison is the cause of most unhappiness. Consider the words of Jack Canfield, "I generally find that comparison is the fast tract to unhappiness." No one ever compares themselves to someone else and comes out even. Nine times out of ten, we compare ourselves to people who are somehow better than us and end up feeling more inadequate." Comparison then becomes the death of happiness. Helen Keller puts it like this, "Instead of comparing our lot with that of those who are more fortunate than we are, we should compare it with the lot of the great majority of our fellow men. It then appears that we are among the privileged." Socrates offers us this wisdom, "If all our misfortunes we laid in one common heap, whence, everyone must take an equal portion, most people would be content to take their own and depart." We must learn to accept ourselves as we are. There is no need to compare our looks or talents with another. We are unique individuals as God has made us special. Max Ehrmann said, "If you compare yourself with others, you may become vain or bitter, for always there will be greater and lesser persons than yourself." Sometimes we look at others and wish we could be them and they, in turn, may be wishing they could be us. We envy another person's job, and that person may be wishing he or she had your job! Princess Anne of England once observed, "I'd like to be a truck driver. I'd think you could run your life that way. It wouldn't be such a bad way of doing it. It would offer a chance to be alone." Somehow we think others are a lot happier than we are. We try to compare ourselves to them and we fall short in our minds and then become discontented. An anonymous writer once said, "What makes us discontented with our condition is the absurdly exaggerated idea we have of the happiness of others."

We can never satisfy all our wants. I love Ralph Waldo Emerson's observations: "There are three wants which can never be satisfied: that of the rich, who want something more, that of the sick who want something different, and that of the traveler, who says, 'Anywhere but not here.'" Being content with what you have is very important as our wants can be limitless. Goethe is credited with saying, "Happy the man who early learns the wide chasm that lies between his wishes and his powers."

Ben Franklin had this to say about happiness, "The U. S. Constitution doesn't guarantee happiness, only the pursuit of it. You have to catch up with it yourself." Martha Washington put it this way, "I am determined to be cheerful and happy in whatever situation I may find myself. For I have learned that the greater part of our misery or unhappiness is determined not by our circumstances but by our disposition."

"Most people are searching for happiness. They're looking for it. They are trying to find it in someone or something outside of themselves. That's a fundamental mistake. Happiness is something that you are, and it comes from the way you think."
-Wayne Dyer

There we have it; happiness is an inside job! It is governed by our mental attitude. It's not circumstances that make us happy, but a certain set of attitudes. Being happy doesn't mean everything is perfect. It means that you've decided to look beyond the imperfections. Your happiness depends on your skill in accepting things as they are. The happiest people don't have the best of everything, they just make the best of everything. You create happiness by the thoughts you put into your mind. Two thousand years ago, Epictetus said, "The essence of philosophy is that a man should so live that his happiness shall depend on little as possible on external things."

I believe learning to be happy is a skill that can be developed. Happiness occurs between the ears in our mind. We need to make up our mind and decide that we are going to be happy and then we need to act happy. Happiness is a choice and it requires effort on our part. It is a by-product of our thoughts and the amount of happiness we experience depends upon the quality of our thoughts. Happiness, then, is a choice.

"When I was five years old, my mother always told me that happiness was the key to life. When I went to school, they asked me what I wanted to be when I grew up. I wrote down 'happy'. They told me I didn't understand the assignment, and I told them they didn't understand life."
-John Lennon

Having a sense of purpose is another way to happiness and the true meaning of life. If you have passion for your work, you'll never work a day in your life. To keep your job interesting, you need to change when change is required, and we must vary our tasks from time to time. Your work is not just a way to make a living…it's an opportunity to make a life. It is vitally important to have a purpose and to stay busy. George Bernard Shaw said, "The only way to avoid being miserable is not to have enough leisure to wonder whether you are happy or not."

Happiness does not just happen; we have to work at it. It is a shedding process. We need to get rid of fear, worry and anxiety and we need to learn how to handle adversity and to accept the things we cannot change. Epictetus conveys this message, "There is only one way to happiness, and that is to cease worrying about things which are beyond the power of our will." Abraham Lincoln put it this way, "Do not worry; eat three square meals a day; say your prayers; be courteous to your creditors; keep your digestion good; exercise; go slow and easy. Maybe there are other things your special case requires to make you happy; but, my friend, these I reckon will give you a good lift." It appears that happiness comes from common blessings. Choose peaceful loving thoughts. Make a decision to act happy and count your blessings. See yourself being happy and it will be just a matter of time before you are happy. Consciously program your mind for happiness. I like what Dr. James W. Parker said about happiness, "Entertain only thoughts that contribute to your happiness. Hate does not make you happy, so do not entertain this thought. Hate does not hurt the person, place, or thing hated. Fear does not make you happy, so do not entertain fear. Fear only upsets the nervous system. Worry does not make you happy, so do not entertain worry. Worry does not improve your future; it not only hampers your ability to think clearly and solve whatever problem you're worrying about, but has many other destructive ramifications."

Service to others is a way to genuine happiness. It makes us feel good when we can help another person. Albert Schweitzer is credited with saying, "I don't know what your destiny will be, but one thing I do know: the only ones among you who will be really happy are those who have sought and found how to serve." Think about that. We need to get our minds off our self and our problems and to think about and to help others. It is truly more blessed to give than to receive. An excellent way to serve is to volunteer your services to others. You can help out at church, schools, senior centers and programs for disadvantaged children, for example. All help is appreciated and it does more for you than the recipient. Strive to make others happy.

Our happiness depends on how we view the world and events. Happiness depends on us thinking in a certain way. Our glass can either be half full or half empty depending how you look at it. We can program ourselves to be happy as it is a learned experience. Learning how to be happy is a skill. It's all about how we teach ourselves to think. It's an inside job. We are as happy as we make up our minds to be. Success and riches will not make us happy; getting married will not make us happy. We will only be happy to the degree that we decide to be happy. As Leo Tolstoy tells us, "Happiness does not depend on outward things, but on the way, we see them." And in a similar vein, Wayne Dyer said, "It is not what is in the world that determines the quality of your life; it is how you choose to process your world in your thoughts." Think of happiness and you'll become happier. Happiness is a habit and the more we practice it the happier we will be. If we act happy, we will be happier. You can teach yourself to be happy. The happiness of your life depends on the quality of your thoughts.

I believe that happiness comes when we learn to appreciate the common simple things in life…a stunning sunset or sunrise, the glimpse of a deer or rabbit while taking a walk, the sound of birds outside your window, the feeling of wind on your face, or the joy of being with grandchildren. Just a note…being a grandparent is the reward you get for not murdering your own children! Happiness comes when we settle in and unwind with a good book or a good movie. It's good to minimize television viewing as all the ads tend to make us unsatisfied if we don't have what is being advertised and all the drug ads are enough to make one sick.

Being cheerful helps a person to bear his burdens and overcome his obstacles. Happiness finds us when we develop a passion for our work, play and adventure. It also comes when we anticipate impending events and the expectation of good.

Happiness can come from doing little things such as writing a letter to a long-time friend or making a call to someone dear to make both you and the recipient feel good for many days. Recall little victories and accomplishments as you focus on what's going well in your life. During up times we need to show gratitude; during down times we need to demonstrate patience. Not all times are happy times as there are times of sadness as well. Carl Jung suggests, "The word 'happiness' would lose its meaning if it were not balanced by sadness."

Multiple studies have shown married people in a long term committed relationship are two times more happy than non-married people. They also tend to suffer less stress and live longer with fewer diseases. As Johann Wolfgang von Goethe put it, "He is happiest, being king or peasant, who finds peace in his home."

Delay retirement for as long as possible. Working longer increases your happiness and will increase the length of your life as well. Working tends to keep us fit, both mentally and physically. It also keeps one in contact with people, especially younger people. Continuing to work also provides some extra income so you can enjoy life more. It's fun to spend money on something you enjoy, whether it be for a trip, a movie or a Coke float.

Another way to increase your well-being and happiness is to keep in contact with family and friends. If you haven't loved, you have not lived. It is extremely important to avoid toxic people and toxic relationships as well. Consider these words of Vanilla Ice, "One thing I didn't understand in life was that I had a hundred million dollars in the bank and I couldn't buy happiness. I had everything: mansions, yachts, Ferraris, Lamborghinis, but I was depressed. I didn't know where I fitted in, but then I found family and friends and I learned the value of life."

"To be happy, take things
as they come and let them
go just as they came."
-Confucius

Just Perfect
"There was a 92-year-old lady who was moving into a nursing home. As she was being wheeled down the corridor, the attendant began to describe the room. "I love it," the old lady gushed. "But you haven't even seen the room yet," the attendant reminded her. "That doesn't have anything to do with it," she replied. "Happiness is something you decide on ahead of time."
-Anonymous

"There are three things you
need to be happy: you need
a faith to live by, a self to
live with and a purpose to
live for."
-Reverend Bob Harrington

The Way to Happiness

Keep your heart free from hate,
your mind from worry.
Live simply, expect little, give much.
Fill your life with love. Scatter sunshine.
Forget self, think of others. Do as you would be done by."
-Norman Vincent Peale

The Path to Happiness
By: William Feather

"Learn to like what doesn't cost much.
Learn to like trees, fields, woods, brooks, fishing, rowing, and hiking.

Learn to like reading, conversation, and music.

Learn to like gardening, carpentering, puttering around the house and lawn and automobile.

Learn to like the song of birds, the companionship of dogs, the laughter and gaiety of children.

Learn to like work and enjoy the satisfaction of doing your job well as it can be done.

Learn to like the sunrise and the sunset, the beating of rain on roof and windows, and the gently fall of snow on a

Dr. Myren D. Anderson
winter day.

Learn to like the mystery of women.
Learn to like them for those ways that
are so different from your own.

Learn to like plain food, plain service,
plain cooking.

Learn to like people, even though some
of them may be different from you.

Learn to like life for its own sake.
Learn to like to be alive.

Learn to keep your wants simple.
Refuse to be owned and anchored by
things and by the opinions of others. That
is the path to happiness."

"The search for happiness is one of the chief
sources of unhappiness."
-Eric Hoffer

"Happiness is like a cat. If you try to coax it or call it, it will avoid
you. It will never come, but if you pay no attention to it and go
about your business, you'll find it rubbing up against your legs and
jumping into your lap."
-William J. Bennett

"Happiness? A good cigar, a good meal, and a good woman-or a
bad woman; it depends on how much happiness you can handle."
-George Burns

TAKEAWAY: SO MUCH OF OUR HAPPINESS DEPENDS ON

HOW WE CHOOSE TO LOOK AT THE WORLD.

"It is possible that our children, our husband, our wife, do not hunger for bread, do not need clothes, do not lack a house. But are we equally sure that none of them feels alone, abandoned, neglected, needing some affection?
That, too, is poverty.
-Mother Teresa

"He is happiest, be he king or peasant, who finds peace in his home."
-Johann Wolfgang von Goethe

30

NO SUCCESS IN LIFE CAN COMPENSATE FOR FAILURE IN THE HOME

Earl Nightingale said, "Success is the progressive realization of a worthy goal or idea." According to Rev. Bob Harrington, there are six main areas for our lives to be in balance: physical health, mental health, spiritual, social, financial and family. You may be highly successful in the first five areas but if your family life is less than ideal, I don't think you have been successful.

George Horace Lorimer said, "It's good to have money and all the things that money can buy; but it's good, too, to check up once in a while and make sure that you haven't lost the things that money can't buy." This would include the love of your husband/wife and the respect and admiration of your children. If we are to be successful in our marriage, we must devote much energy and love for our mate. It is the number one priority. The best thing a parent can do for their children is to love their spouse. If the marriage is sound, the children will grow up in a pleasant stable environment and learn to love unconditionally. Frederick Douglass said, "It is easier to build strong children than to repair broken men."

It seems that most married couples know what to do to keep their spouse happy and content, but somehow, we forget and take our husband or wife for granted. Frederick Bailes hit the nail on the head when he said, "Thoughtlessness has killed love in the hearts of more women than infidelity." Husbands and wives (like puppies) feel what you feel. Cavett Robert said, "Everybody has a big sign on them that says, "Make me feel important." Feeling needed and being appreciated is a basic need. An anonymous writer said, "Besides, positive strokes in our lives help us to feel energized." Friedrich Nietzsche said, "It is not a lack of love, but a lack of friendship that makes unhappy marriages."

It is interesting to note love is between like and lust in the dictionary. People must get what they want from a relationship; if they don't get it, they will go somewhere else. The relationship is either evolving or dissolving. Caring plus sharing and giving plus loving equals living. Leo Buscaglia said, "I have a very strong feeling that the opposite of love is not hate, it's apathy. It's not giving a damn." If you miss love, you miss life. Someone once said, "Marriage is a fifty/fifty proposition. The husband tells his wife what to do…and the wife tells him where to go!" In reality marriage is a hundred/hundred proposition. Always remember people do things for their reasons and those reasons are emotionally based. Success in marriage is a lot more than just finding the right person; it's a matter of being the right person. Couples can fall out of love and back in love many times in a marriage.

Centuries ago, Homer had this to say about marriage, "There is nothing nobler or more admirable than when two people who see eye to eye keep house as man and wife, confounding their enemies and delighting their friends." On a humorous note, they say you should never ask your wife why she married you…she's probably asking herself the same question! Every marriage has some "ups and downs" at times but it's important to communicate with your spouse to work out any differences. An elderly lady was asked how they managed to stay together for 65 years, the woman replied, "We were born in a time when if something was broken, you fixed it… not throw it away." Many people always think the grass is greener on the other side of the fence. Dr. John DeMartini tells us about the law of one and the many, "When you are single and date the many, you are looking for the one. When you are married and you have the one, you wonder about the many!" So, do not spoil what you have by desiring what you have not.

Charles E. "Tremendous" Jones said that, "Commitment in marriage is more important than love, commitment will save your marriage when your love dies or until it lives again." He also said, "Commit your life to your marriage…not to your mate." H. Jackson Brown Jr. said, "Remember that creating a successful marriage is like farming: you have to start over again every morning." George Bernard Shaw humorously remarked, "Marriage is an alliance entered into by a man who can't sleep with the window shut, and a woman who can't sleep with the window open." You must work to create rapport with your mate, for without it, good communication cannot take place. Communication is vital in a marriage. It's always good to use your spouse's name frequently…not just when you're mad. Helen Rowland said, "To be happy with a man you must understand him a lot and love him, a little; to be happy with a woman you must love her a lot and not try to understand her at all."

It is important that husbands appreciate all the things their wives do for them. A wife is not just a wife; she is a loving companion, a lover, a cook, a seamstress, a housekeeper, a financial planner, a mother, the number one teacher of our children and the list goes on. William James said, "The deepest principle of human nature is a craving to be appreciated."

A wife needs acceptance. approval, recognition and praise. A wife must not be criticized or she will become defensive. Never keep a record of wrongs. Most wives spend their lives being discounted. A woman feels the most anxiety and hostility just prior to the beginning of her period. A basic need for a woman is conversation. Women need to talk two times more than men. Eye contact is important so talk to her, not at her. Wives can be bored with their routine or stressed from their work outside the home. Mothers can be stressed out from the children and may have feelings of isolation and loneliness, especially if they are a stay at home mom.

It is helpful to take your wife out for dinner or lunch every week. Flowers will help to cheer up a woman. They say that "If you treat your wife as a thoroughbred, she'll never turn into a nag." It is helpful to romance your wife with love notes, flowers and unexpected gifts, etc. We don't tend to remember days…we remember moments. We should have a goal to have 60 minutes of quality time with our wife each day. Most people do not get that much time in a week. Ten second hugs and ten second kisses are also helpful. Little sentences like, "You're not fat," "I love you," "You are so sexy" and "Let's eat out," will help to keep the marriage healthy. Other good ideas include having a date night every week and a getaway weekend each month. A husband must never compare his wife to his mother. Joyce Kimball said the following turns women off:

Criticism
Yelling at her
Being ridiculed or made fun of
Being talked down to
Name calling
Being ignored (if you ignore her now, she'll ignore you later)
Not keeping your word
An unclean body
Not being a leader

The family unit is only as strong as the father. Be a strong decision maker, but admit it when you are wrong. It is the husband's job to be a good provider and it is his job to protect and lead the family. There's an old saying that "The man makes the living but the woman makes the living worthwhile." Perhaps, in this day and age the roles could be reversed. If a wife is working outside the home, the husband must help with the children and housework. A husband must be patient because his wife is most likely stressed out from work. It is the husband's duty to cheer up his wife and to make her like herself more. Your wife will become what you think of her. How would I like to be married to me? That's a question every married person should ask themselves. Men need to have quiet time when they get home from work. They need to be appreciated for what they do… and don't do.

A basic need for a husband is a recreational companion…also sexual fulfillment, admiration by his wife and domestic support. A husband values his wife for how she makes him feel. Husbands need to learn how to communicate their needs so they get what they want out of life. Like wives, husbands need acceptance, approval, recognition and appreciation.

Make a list of your partner's good qualities. Give your attention and devotion to them. To the world you may be just one person…but to your spouse, you may be the world. Encourage your spouse. Every home needs an encourager. A word of encouragement from a spouse can save a marriage. It has been said that "Encouragement is oxygen for the soul." If you are wrong, admit it and move on. Peter Marshall offers this bit of wisdom. "Lord, where we are wrong, make us willing to change; where we are right, make us easy to live with." Apologize when you need to; it shows you value your relationship more than your ego. Learn to keep your mouth shut at the right time. Silence is golden. Look at things from a spouse's point of view and consider their needs and desires.

Marriage is like a two-way street. There has to be give and take. Your soulmate has positive and negative qualities; they are in balance. We need to accentuate the positive and overlook the negative qualities. Leo Tolstoy said, "What counts in making a happy marriage is not so much how compatible you are but how you deal with incompatibility." Never depend on your spouse for approval or happiness. Depend on yourself for your sense of self-worth and well-being. Become thick skinned so little irritations don't bother you so much. The only person you can ever change is you…so work on yourself. If you are waiting for your spouse to get better, you are trying to correct the wrong person. Your spouse needs to feel that "When I am with you, I like myself better."

Admit it when you make a mistake; do not defend wrongs. Fidelity in marriage is a must. The best thing to give your mate is love and faithfulness. It's hard to trust someone the second time around after they already gave you a reason not to trust them. Ann Landers said, "If you marry a man who cheats on his wife, you'll be married to a man who cheats on his wife." I believe Dr. Joyce Brothers gave the best marital advice. She said, "Someone has to give way. There is a rule in sailing that the more maneuverable ship should give way to the less maneuverable craft. I think this is sometimes a good rule to follow in human relationships, as well." Dr. John D. DeMartini said, "Give space and you get love; give love and you get space." He also said, "If you think something will give you more positives than negatives, you're living with an illusion. When you get what you imagine you want, you'll find out that it comes with a catch or a twist that you didn't anticipate. You only get a new set of pains and pleasures."

I believe this pertains to marriage in particular. There are many positives and negatives in marriage as people are very complex. It is important you allow your spouse the complete freedom to be themselves. Accept them without trying to change them. Become a good finder rather than a fault finder. Common everyday courtesy helps to improve a marriage. Use "please" and "thank you" frequently. Pass food, salt and pepper to your partner at meal time. A man should walk on the outside of the sidewalk. He should open the car door for his wife, hold a chair for her and help her with her coat. These are small things but they help to keep love alive, as well as showing respect as a gentleman. Unexpected gifts are always welcome as are compliments. Say "I love you" often.

All married couples should read a good book about sex. Ann Landers said, "Men are like microwave ovens; women are crock pots sexually." Men are more visual and easily aroused; a woman must be conditioned. A husband must cultivate love for his wife all day as a woman simmers throughout the day; usually they are not as spontaneous. The best sex in marriage takes place when both partners feel loved and are sure that they are not only accepted but respected. Robert A. Heinlein quotes, "Sex without love is merely healthy exercise." To improve a couple's sex life, the wife needs to initiate love-making sometimes. She also needs to be creative and be able to try new positions. Husbands need to bring a clean body to bed and they need to be attentive to their wives' needs. Men tend to want to sleep after sex but women need to lay together, talk and fall asleep close. Good conversation leads to good sex. Ann Landers said, "Women complain about sex more often than men. Their gripes fall into two main categories: 1. Not enough, 2. Too much." She also said, "A woman gives sex to get love; a man gives love to get sex."

As a husband, how long has it been since you said something nice about your wife's body? Do you remember to compliment her on her hairstyle or her perfume? Have you given her a full body hug lately? How about a back or foot rub? Have you praised her for anything lately? People value you for how you make them feel. Most people flourish with praise.

As a wife, when was the last time you complimented your husband on anything? Have you ever complimented him on being faithful? When was the last time you met your husband at the door with only your negligee on when he came home from work? Zsa Zsa Gabor said, "Husbands are like fires, they go out if unattended." She also said, "A man is incomplete until he's married…and then he's finished!" The best time to express love for your mate is before someone else does. You need to tend your garden, as they say. Love-making is a lot more likely if you live in harmony. Dale Carnegie said it best, "If you want to gather honey, don't kick over the beehive." Rodney Dangerfield had this to say, "Never tell your wife she is lousy in bed. She'll go out and get a second opinion."

In any relationship there are bound to be disagreements and hurt feelings. A healthy argument can clear the air but it has to be fair. Silent treatment, withholding sex, criticism, physical abuse, name calling, etc., damage the relationship, perhaps fatally. If arguments occur, they must not occur in front of the children as the egos of children do not grow in hostile environments. One of the best things we can do for a child is set a good example. The question must be asked, do I want to be right or do I want to be happy? A timeout changes the situation. Go for a walk and cool off. Know when to keep your mouth shut. Learn to forgive and forget. The Scriptures say, "Don't let the sun go down on your anger." Many marriages suffer from a communication deficit.

Charles "Tremendous" Jones said, "Some people die strangers after living together for thirty years." In an age where 50 percent of marriages end in divorce, it seems that more communication is needed. Most people with a problem or complaint don't want a solution, they just want you to listen. Listening helps your spouse feel good and makes them feel valued. Perhaps just listening may help more than you will ever know. Consider the words of Laurence J. Peter, "Speak when you are angry and you will make the best speech you'll ever regret." It has been said by Washington Irving that, "A sharp tongue is the only tool that grows keener with constant use." It's good to remember we communicate 7% through words, 38% how you say the words (tone) and 55% through our body language. Your spouse can feel your attitude.

People radiate "feeling" to the subconscious mind of another. Ignoring a person is a great insult and must be avoided. An apology is always welcomed and appreciated. Marlene Dietrich observed, "Once a woman has forgiven her man, she must not reheat his sins for breakfast." Never be reluctant to say "I love you" and remember…a touch is worth a thousand words. Touch your spouse with a loving hand at least once a day. Don't expect your spouse to be perfect. We all have some dysfunctional programming. We all make mistakes, so learn and practice the fine art of forgiveness. Love is seeing good in another person. Always avoid the mad-sad-shout-pout disease (I'm going to get mad so you have to do something to make me glad). Maxwell Maltz said, "Take the trouble to stop and think of the other person's feelings, his viewpoints, his desires and needs. Think more of what the other fellow wants, and how he must feel." To handle yourself, use your head; to handle others, use your heart. Maya Angelou put it like this, "People will forget what you said, people will forget what you did, but people will never forget how you made them feel." Courtship after marriage is vital for a tranquil marriage. An unknown author provided a short course in human relations:

The six most important words: "I admit I made a mistake"…The five most important words: "You did a good job"…The four most important words: "What is your opinion?"…The three most important words: "If you please"…The two most important words: "Thank you"…The one most important word" "We"…The least important word: "I."

Children are just like us, only shorter. They need recognition, approval, acceptance and praise just like adults do. It is important to praise any action you wish to see repeated. Concentrate on what they do right. Common courtesies like "please" and "thank you" set a good example and teach children to respond similarly. It is important to take your children with you on vacation. They will learn more than at school, but more importantly, they actually feel like they are an integral part of the family. Little gifts, a pat on the back and a kind word can work wonders. Avoid making careless promises. Do what you say you are going to do. Talk to your children about small concerns so they talk to you when the big ones come up later on. It is not an easy job to be a parent as we must learn on the job. If your small child writes "I love you" on the wall with crayons, do you scold them for writing on the wall or do you hug them for saying, "I love you?" Consider the words of Confucius, "Govern a family as you would cook a small fish---very gently." Make allowances for inexperience in children. Is it irresponsibility or on purpose? Josh Billings had this advice, "To bring up a child in the way he should go, travel that way yourself once in a while." People, including children, will never forget criticism and compliments. Dave Willis is credited with saying, "Husbands, love your wives well! Your children are noticing how you treat her. You are teaching your sons how they should treat women and you are teaching your daughters what they should expect from men."

H. Jackson Brown Jr. put it like this, "Live so that when your children think of fairness, caring, and integrity, they think of you." The family is under attack from many angles in today's society. Drug use, alcoholism, domestic abuse and high divorce rates all contribute to less than desirable family life. Another thing that's harmful to family life is the overemphasis on athletic events which start in grade school and continue into high school. Families don't have time to eat together as one parent goes with one child to their event and the other parent takes another child to another event in opposite directions. James Dobson summed it up like this, "What is the biggest obstacle facing the family right now? It is over commitment, time pressure. There is nothing that will destroy family life more insidiously than hectic schedules and busy lives, where spouses are too exhausted to communicate, too worn out to have sex, too fatigued to talk to the kids. That frantic lifestyle is just as destructive as one involving outbroken sin. If Satan can't make you sin, he'll make you busy, and that's just about the same thing." Socrates spoke of the dangers of a busy life a couple thousand years ago, as well, "Beware the barrenness of a busy life." It's important that parents keep a balance between work and the family. Charles "Tremendous" Jones said, "Never put family ahead of work and never put work ahead of family." The following are a few quotes about love, family life and marriage:

"There is no greater happiness for a man than approaching a door at the end of a day knowing someone on the other side of the door is waiting for the sound of his footsteps."
-Ronald Reagan

"Keep your eyes wide open before marriage, and half shut afterwards."
-Benjamin Franklin

"Choose your life's mate carefully. From this one decision will come 90 percent of all your happiness or misery."
-H. Jackson Brown, Jr.

"Women and cats will do as they please and men and dogs should relax and get used to the idea."
- Robert A. Heinlein

"By all means marry. If you get a good wife, you'll become happy; if you get a bad one, you'll become a philosopher."
-Socrates (470-399 B.C.)

"Of all the pleasures of marriage, friendship has got to be one of the best. Two hands, intertwined until the end of time…Doesn't get much better than that."
-Fawn Weaver

"God gave women intuition and femininity. Used properly, the combination easily jumbles the brain of any man I've ever met."
- Farrah Fawcett

"Remember that children, marriages, and flower gardens reflect the kind of care they get."
-H. Jackson Brown Jr.

"Woman was created from the rib of man. She was not made from his head to top him, nor out of his feet to be trampled upon, but out of his side, to be equal to him, under his arm to be protected, and near his heart to be loved."
-Matthew Henry

"No matter how happily a woman may be married, it always pleases her to discover that there is a nice man who wishes that she were not."
-H.L. Mencken

"Love is composed of a single soul inhabiting two bodies."
-Aristotle

"I hate to be a failure. I hate and regret the failure of my marriages. I would gladly give all my millions for just one lasting marital success."
-J. Paul Getty

THOU SHALT NOT KILL

"Yesterday I killed…my son's joy…in the victory of his team. I complained about his dirty clothes—torn at the seam. The day before I killed my daughter's pride in that dress she'd made. I pointed out its faults, then added faint praise. One day I killed a friendship—

turned affection to hate. I misunderstood that's all—but it was too late. I killed my spouse's love. Not with a mighty blow. It died bit by bit; year by year…so slow. Tonight I saw the light of love die slowly in her look; when she reached toward me with her hand…and I picked up…a book. Oh God of the resurrection…take me by the hand. And teach me how to truly love and love to understand."
-Edith Wyvell

>Your children are not your children.
They are the sons and daughters of life's longing for itself.
They come through you but not from you.
And though they are with you yet they belong not to you.
You may give them your love but not your thoughts.
For they have their thoughts.
You may house their bodies but not their souls.
For their soul's dwell in the house of tomorrow, which you cannot visit, not even in your dreams.
You may strive to be like them, but seek not make them like you.
For life goes not backward nor tarries with yesterday.
You are the bows from which your children as living arrows are sent forth.
-Kahlil Gibran

I WISH MY DADDY WAS A DOG

One day when Bruce was just a lad first starting out in school,
he came into my workshop and climbed upon a stool.
I saw him as he entered but I hadn't time to play,
so I merely nodded to him and said, "Don't get in the way."
He sat a while just thinking…as quiet as could be,
then carefully he got down and came and stood by me.
He said, "Old Shep, he never works and he has lots of fun.
He runs around the meadows and barks up at the sun.
He chases after rabbits and always scares the cats.
He likes to chew on old shoes and sometimes Mother's hats.
But when we're tired of running and we sit down on a log,
I sometimes get to thinking…I wish my Daddy was a dog.
Cause then when I come home from school he'd run and lick my

hand, and we would jump and holler and tumble in the sand.
And then I'd be happy as happy as could be,
'cause we would play the whole day through just my Dad and me.
Now I know you work real hard to buy us food and clothes,
and you need to get the girls those fancy ribbons and bows,
but sometimes when I'm lonesome I think 'twould be lots of fun,
if my Daddy was a dog, and all his work was done."
Now when he'd finished speaking he looked so lonely there'
I reached out my hand to him and ruffled up his hair.
And as I turned my head aside to brush away a tear,
I thought how nice it was to have my Son so near.
I know the Lord didn't mean for man to toil his
whole life through,
"Come on, my Son, I'm sure I have some time for you."
You should have seen the joy and sunlight in his eye,
as we went outside to play…just my Son and I.
Now, as the years have flown and youth has slipped away,
I've tried always to remember to allow some time to play.
When I pause to reminisce and think of joys and strife,
I carefully turn the pages of this wander's book of life.
I find the richest entry recorded in this daily log,
is the day that small boy whispered, "I wish my Daddy was a dog."
- Elrod C. Leany

He stopped to pat a small dog's head,
A little thing to do;
And yet the dog, remembering,
Was glad the whole day through.
He gave a rose into the hand
Of one who loved it much;
'Twas just a rose, but ah, the job
That lay in its soft touch.
He spoke a word so tenderly---
A word's a wee small thing;
And yet it stirred a weary heart
to hope again and sing.
-Author unknown

CHILDREN LEARN WHAT THEY LIVE

If a child lives with criticism,
He learns to condemn.
If a child lives with hostility,
He learns to fight.
If a child lives with ridicule,
He learns to be shy.
If a child lives with shame,
He learns to feel guilty.
If a child lives with tolerance,
He learns to be patient.
If a child lives with encouragement,
He learns confidence.
If a child lives with praise,
He learns to appreciate.
If a child lives with fairness,
He learns justice.
If a child lives with security,
He learns to have faith.
If a child lives with approval,
He learns to like himself.
If a child lives with acceptance and friendship.
He learns to find love in the world.
-Dorothy Law Nolte

TAKEAWAY: IF YOU LOSE LOVE, YOU LOSE LIFE.

Dr. Myren D. Anderson

"Forgiveness is the way to true health and happiness." -Gerald Jampolsky

"Neither do I condemn thee; go and sin no more."
-Jesus

31

A GREAT LIFE REQUIRES A LOT OF FORGIVENESS

In order to be a forgiving person, we must be able to forgive ourselves and others. Many people beat themselves up due to actual or perceived wrong doings they may have committed at some point in their life. We have all done things that have caused us guilt. Guilt is a strong emotion that keeps us tied to the past and causes us to feel less deserving. The more we think of some wrongdoing, the more guilt we accumulate. It's counterproductive. It is imperative that we learn to forgive ourselves because if we can't, we will never be able to forgive others. As Cicero beseeches, "Let us not listen to those who think we ought to be angry with our enemies, and who believe this to be great and manly. Nothing is so praiseworthy, nothing so clearly shows a great and noble soul, as clemency and readiness to forgive." And Aristotle said, "The high minded man does not bear grudges, for it is not the mark of a great soul to remember injuries, but to forget them."

Perhaps, one of the greatest acts of forgiveness occurred when Pope John Paul II visited his attacker in jail and forgave him. The Pope was shot in the abdomen, lost much of his blood and had to endure a five-hour surgery. As Saint Francis of Assisi said, "It is in pardoning that we are pardoned." Forgiveness is one of man's greatest achievements. It frees us from hate, anger and resentment and gives us inner peace. As Catherine Ponder put it so succinctly, "When you hold resentment toward another you are bound to that person or condition by an emotional link that is stronger than steel. Forgiveness is the only way to resolve that link and get free."

We have all been hurt by another person, perhaps your wife or husband, a parent or even a complete stranger, and in the larger scheme of things it was miniscule but we thought about it a lot and it became bigger and bigger in our minds. It would have been much better to have shrugged it off and to have forgiven the person. It's even worse when someone we dislike commits a wrongful act or says something to us that hurts. Holding on to these hurts or perceived wrongs tends to keep us stuck. Here's what Ann Landers wrote in one of her columns, "Resentment is letting someone you despise live rent-free in your head." Don't take yourself or others too seriously. Be too big to be resentful. Forgive all those who have harmed or slighted you and forgive yourself for the same offenses that you may have committed. We need to be insensitive to the imperfections of ourselves and others. So let us strive to be more forgiving. It will help us to live happy and healthy lives. Many physical and psychosomatic disorders occur in people who are unable to forgive. Here is how Catherine Ponder phrased it, "Forgiveness is all powerful. Forgiveness heals all ills." She also said, "The forgiving state of mind is a magnetic power for attracting good." Being able to forgive is a mark of a Christian. Christians are not perfect, but they are forgiving. Above all, do not hate. I think Martin Luther King Jr. said it best. He said, "Nothing that a man does, takes him lower than when he hates." Mahatma Gandhi said, "An eye for an eye only makes the whole world blind."

So forgive yourself and forgive others. Forgiveness is an act of self-love and the love and acceptance of others. If you forgive, you will help to rid yourself of guilt, depression, anger and resentment and you will develop more compassion and understanding. It might be helpful to create a list of the people you need to forgive. A wonderful affirmation that you can repeat over and over is, "I forgive those who have harmed me; I forgive myself for having harmed others." Grant yourself and others forgiveness and complete absolution. Marianne Williamson said, "Forgiveness is not always easy. At times, it feels more painful than the wound we suffered, to forgive the one that inflicted it. And yet, there is no peace without forgiveness."

"To be wronged is nothing unless you continue to remember it."
Confucius

"One of the secrets of a
Long and fruitful life is to
Forgive everybody everything
Every night before you go to bed."
-Bernard Baruch

"If thy brother wrongs thee,
Remember not so much his
Wrong-doing, but more than
Ever that he is thy brother."
-Epictetus

"One of the most lasting pleasures you can experience is the feeling that comes over you when you genuinely forgive an enemy-whether he knows it or not."
-O.A. Battista

"Here is a mental treatment that is guaranteed to cure every ill that flesh is heir to: Sit for a half-hour every night and mentally forgive everyone against whom you have any ill will or antipathy."
-Charles Fillmore

"Make allowances for each other's faults, and forgive anyone who offends you. Remember the Lord forgave you, so
you must forgive."
-Colossians 3:13

On a humorous note, this is what Elmo Phillips had to say about forgiveness:
"When I was a kid I used
to pray every night for a new
bicycle. Then I realized that
the Lord doesn't work that way
so I stole one and asked
Him to forgive me."

TAKEAWAY: FORGIVING OURSELVES AND OTHERS FREES US AND GIVES US PEACE.

Dr. Myren D. Anderson

"Life isn't about waiting for the storm to pass.
It's about learning to dance in the rain."
-Vivian Greene

"God gave us the gift of life;
It is up to us to give ourselves the gift of living well." -Voltaire

32

ENJOYING LIFE IS A SKILL…THE ART OF LIVING WELL

Enjoying life is a skill…a skill that can be learned. As one ages, we tend to accept life as it comes, savoring small successes along the way and dealing with adversities as they come. As Virginia Satir observed, "Life is not the way it is supposed to be, it's the way it is. The way you cope with it makes the difference." We eventually realize there is a balance between the good and the not so good and so endeavor to seek an even keel, not getting elated over the good and not getting depressed over the bad. I love Ralph Waldo Emerson's observation, "For everything you missed, you have gained something else, and for everything you gain, you lose something else." One comes to realize you can't take the "hurt" out of life but you can roll with the punches. Pain is inevitable but suffering is optional. We learn to focus more on what we have and not so much on what we don't have.

I think Epictetus said it best, "He is a wise man who does not grieve for the things which he has not, but rejoices for those which he has." Dr. Seuss also said it well when he reminded us to, "Step with care and great tact, and remember that life's a great balancing act." To live a complete, balanced and happy life we need to be content with our status in life. It's good to strive for what we need and want but there comes a time when enough is enough. Some of the happiest people I know do not have a lot of material possessions but are content anyway. Others have great abundance and are still not satisfied as their ego's demand more and more. Consider the words of the great philosopher Socrates, who said, "He is richest who is content with the least." Horace is credited with saying, "You will live wisely if you are happy in your lot."

So, choose to be content today with what you have. Your happiness depends on the quality of your thoughts. Always think positively and try to see the good in daily events. Look for the rainbow after the rain. Feel that each new day is a gift (a miniature life) and that something good is going to happen. Learn to savor life's small pleasures. Live with a grateful heart one day at a time. I think Ziad K. Abdelnour said it best, "Learn to appreciate what you have, before time makes you appreciate what you had." Living well is within everyone's grasp but most people do not make a conscious effort to really enjoy life, they merely exist. Many times, folks are so busy earning a living that they forget to make a life. Parents and teachers should make a special effort to teach their children and students to appreciate life and how to enhance it. Alexander the Great said, "I am indebted to my father for living, but to my teacher for living well." Sadly, most people don't think about their lives until it's late in the game. The French writer Colette said, "What a wonderful life I've had! I only wish I'd realized it sooner."

Every day is a miniature life and each of us needs to be mindful of how brief our lives really are. It behooves us to make the most of each day and live each one to the best of our ability. We need to enjoy the moment and not dwell so much on the future or the past. Enjoy today! Look for happy surprises every day. Dale Carnegie put it this way, "One of the most tragic things I know about human nature is that all of us tend to put off living. We are all dreaming of some magical rose garden over the horizon instead of enjoying the roses that are blooming outside our windows today." An nonymous writer wrote, "First I was dying to finish high school and start college. And then I was dying to finish college and start working. And then I was dying to marry and have children. And then I was dying for my children to grow old enough for school so I could return to work. And then I was dying to retire. And now I am dying and suddenly I realize I forgot to live." The Roman Poet, Horace, offered this wisdom, "Carpe diem! Rejoice while you are alive; enjoy the day; live life to the fullest; make the most of what you have. It is later than you think." It doesn't have to be like this. We can learn to enjoy life more by appreciating each day. Living in the moment (present time consciousness) will enhance our quality of life. Joan Baez had this to say, "You don't get to choose how you're going to die. Or when. You can only decide how you're going to live. Now." Always feel like your best days are before you. Believe that you are in the right place at the right time. Fill your days with fun and meaningful activities. Live in a state of joyful expectancy. Set aside time for meditation and for unexpected and spontaneous activities. Withdraw only positive thoughts from your memory bank…not the negative ones. As Cavett Robert said it so beautifully, "Yesterday is a cancelled check; tomorrow is a promissory note; only today is legal tender, only now is negotiable." Here is how Ralph Waldo Emerson phrased it, "Finish every day and be done with it. You have done what you could. Some blunders and absurdities no doubt crept in; forget them as soon as you can. Tomorrow is a new day."

A great life requires that we practice the joy of giving. Marlo Thomas said, "My father said there were two types of people in the world: givers and takers. The takers may eat better, but the givers sleep better." Winston Churchill offered us this wisdom, "We make a living by what we get, but we make a life by what we give." A warm and generous heart is essential for happiness. As we get older and wiser, I believe we tend to become better givers. We can give of our money and we can give of our time by volunteering for various activities. We can write letters, make a telephone call to a lonely person or visit someone in the hospital, nursing home or jail. All of these activities improve the quality of our lives as well as the recipient. As we get older, we can become better or bitter; the choice is ours. I like the following Prayer from the Catholic Devotional:

> "Dear Lord, teach me to be generous,
> to give and not count the cost,
> to fight and not heed the wounds,
> to work and not ask for no reward,
> save that knowing that I do your will." Amen

As the scriptures remind us, "One man gives freely, yet grows all the richer; another withholds what he should give, and only suffers want. A liberal man will be enriched, and the one who waters will himself be watered." Proverbs 11:24-25

THE LAW OF GIVING AND RECEIVING
By Ernest Holmes

"Everything in nature moves in circles. What goes out must come back. Unless the seed is sown it cannot bear fruit. There must be a planting time for every harvest. Who gives all receives all. Who refuses to give limits the possibility of the greater good returning to him."

"Love and you will be loved. Extend joy and you will become more joyful. The ancient Talmud says, "God will doubly guide the already guided," and Jesus, the greatest of the great, said, "Give, and it shall be given unto you; good measure, pressed down, and shaken together, and running over, shall men give into your bosom. For with the same measure that ye mete withal it shall be measured to you again." (Luke 6:38)

We do not give because God needs the gift but because the giving increases, broadens and deepens the life of the giver. Nor shall we give from the standpoint of duty. The Universe refuses to bargain with us. It already has given us everything it has. But it also has provided that the gift of life can be received in its fullness only as it flows through us to the fullness of others.

How wonderful is this exact balance which God and nature keep; how perfect is the law of God and how glorious the opportunity to join with the Infinite Giver in the givingness of the self to the joy of life!

Life is not a rehearsal; this is it. We can live it well or we can just exist; the choice is up to us."

One day your life will flash before your eyes. Make sure it's worth watching. Some folks are bored their entire life. John Burroughs had a different outlook. He said, "I still find each day too short for all the thoughts I want to think, all the walks I want to take, all the books I want to read, and all the friends I want to see." What a wonderful attitude! We need to live our life in such a way that we don't have any regrets we didn't do something. We don't want to look back and find we have wasted precious years, months, weeks and days and, yes, minutes because we were just drifting along in life. George Bernard Shaw said it like this, "I want to be thoroughly used up when I die, for the harder I work, the more I live. I rejoice in life for its own sake."

I believe we are here on planet earth to learn the lessons of life, that God runs the world and that there are no accidents in the universe. As we get older, we realize it is important to detach ourselves from the affairs of the world. We have peace when we accept life the way it is. It's wise to stay away from "world causes" as they are mostly ego trips. We need to program our own minds rather than be programmed by the world mind. Don't waste your time worrying about what is wrong in the world; enjoy what's right in the world. Know that life is good; in fact, it is a phenomenal trip! Cavett Robert put it this way, "A new day is a gift to be enjoyed…not a sentence to be endured." Long ago, Epictetus stated, "Ask not that events should happen as you will, but let your will be that events should happen as they do, and you shall have peace." It is imperative that we not only make peace with the world, but with ourselves, as well. Reinhold Niebuhr's Serenity Prayer sums it up beautifully, "God grant me the serenity to accept the things I cannot change, courage to change the things I can, and wisdom to know the difference."

Life without humor is like bread without butter. Humor is important at any age, but it is especially important as we get older. Laughter releases endorphins which makes us feel good, helps to reduce stress and relieves pain. It has been said that, "Laughter is God's hand on a troubled world." Mark Twain said, "Humor is mankind's greatest blessing." Henry Ward Beecher offers this bit of wisdom,

"A person without a sense of humor is like a wagon without springs, jolted by every pebble on the road."

Without a doubt, humor enhances our lives. Norman Cousins, who healed himself from ankylosing spondylitis, a crippling disease, with laughter, had this to say, "Hearty laughter is a good way to jog internally without having to go outdoors." Humor helps us to endure life during hard times. It lightens our load and lifts our spirits. Wayne Dyer wrote, "The day is "lousy" or "great" depending upon the judgment you decide to attach to it." God gave us the power to choose. It is up to us to choose happiness and contentment if that is what we want. Your life is a reflection of what you most frequently think about. I like what Wynn Davis had to say about the power of choice, "Our greatest power is the power to choose. We can decide where we are, what we do, and what we think. No one can take the power to choose away from us. It is ours alone. We can do what we want to do. We can be who we want to be." How we look at things determines the quality of our life. The glass is either half full or half empty.

Centuries ago, Marcus Aurelius said, "The happiness of your life depends upon the quality of your thoughts: therefore, guard accordingly, and take care that you entertain no notions unsuitable to virtue and reasonable nature." Consider the words of Sydney J. Harris, "When I hear somebody sigh, 'Life is hard,' I am always tempted to ask, "Compared to what?" Don't focus so much on problems. Always keep hope and enthusiasm alive.

No discussion about living well would be complete without mentioning having and caring for pets, especially dogs and cats. Nothing can change your mood and lift your spirits faster than to be greeted enthusiastically by your dog after a long day. It's fun to see how excited they get when going for a walk and how contented they are when chewing on a bone or just lying by your side. Life is better with a dog. An anonymous writer once wrote, "If you are lucky...a dog will come into your life, steal your heart and change everything." Roger Caras said, "Dogs are not our whole life, but they make our lives whole." Andy Rooney went a step further saying, "The average dog is a nicer person than the average person."

Dogs are loyal, affectionate and will give up their life to protect you. They are truly man's best friend and companion. Perhaps, Josh Billings said it best, "A dog is the only thing on earth that loves you more than you love yourself." Incidentally, "dog" spelled backwards is "God." Another benefit of having a dog is that you need to exercise the dog so you get some exercise yourself. They say that if your dog is fat, you are not getting enough exercise. Andrew Weil, M.D., said, "One of the most obvious ways dogs can improve physical and mental health is via daily walks." Walking the dog gets you outside in nature so you can see the clouds and the trees, feel the wind and listen to the sound of the birds." Experts say only about 50% of people are happy. I believe dog owners are in that 50% group. I have many fond memories of my dog, Molly, a black Labrador. These include watching her do three somersaults in a row, sliding down a snowbank on her back, catching a tennis ball on the run or proudly retrieving a pheasant. Sometimes she lies at my feet dreaming in her sleep with muscles twitching and making little yelp sounds. Molly loves golf balls. She can even find them in tall grass or brush. Sometimes she'll be walking along the ditch alongside the golf course and will stop and sniff a few times and frantically start digging and soon comes up with a golf ball! My son had a dog named Ally that would get her food dish when hungry and open the refrigerator and get him a beer. She would also shut off the lights when they left the apartment. They would go to McDonald's, and each would have a cheeseburger.

Cats make excellent pets, as well, but they tend to be more reserved in manner. Alfred North Whitehead humorously spoke of the difference between cats and dogs. "If a dog jumps into your lap it is because he is fond of you: but if a cat does the same thing it is because your lap is warmer." Lewis Grizzard put it like this, "You call to a dog and a dog will break its neck to get to you. Dogs just want to please. Call to a cat and its attitude is, "What's in it for me?" A cat's purring is very relaxing and watching a cat chase after a toy and pounce on it is fun and entertaining. A cat's gracefulness is unparalleled in the animal world. Leonardo da Vinci said, "The smallest feline is a masterpiece." Pam Brown said, "Kittens are wide-eyed, soft and sweet, with needles in their jaws and feet." Abraham Lincoln made this observation, "No matter how much cats fight, there always seem to be plenty of kittens." Animals teach children how to love. Anatole France observed, "Until one has loved an animal, a part of one's soul remains unawakened."

If we meet life with an enthusiastic attitude, we will get better at living the longer we live. Each day is a miniature lifetime, so we need to live everyday well. Everyday is a miracle. Don't dwell on what you have lost as you get older; instead dwell on what you have left. Perhaps, the best is yet to be. Continue to strengthen your life urges and weaken your death urges. Have expectations of better health, increased vitality, and greater longevity as you age. Our goal should be a victorious and triumphant life. Henri Frederic Amiel said, "To know how to grow old is the masterwork of wisdom, and one of the most difficult chapters in the great art of living."

It's important we don't get accustomed to the miracles that happen to each of us every day. This is how Albert Einstein put it, "There are two ways to live; you can live as if nothing is a miracle; you can live as if everything is a miracle." One of the tragedies of life is that we tend to take too many things for granted and we don't really appreciate life for what it is. We don't really appreciate our health until it starts to fail. We may not really appreciate our work until we retire and then we miss the "good old days." We can be so busy with day to day life that we don't enjoy our spouse or children as much as we should either. As Horace said, "He who postpones the hour of living is like the rustic who waits for the river to run out before he crosses."

"For a long time, it had seemed to me that life was about to begin-real life. But there was always some obstacle in the way. Something to be got through first, some unfinished business, time still to be served, a debt to be paid. Then life would begin. At last it dawned on me that these obstacles were my life." -Anonymous

Ed Foreman offers us this wisdom, "The tragedy of life is not that it ends so soon, but that we wait so long to begin it." Mae West summed it up like this, "Life is a banquet and most people are starving to death."

We need to slow down to enjoy life more thoroughly. Some folks are so busy with meetings, social activities, political activities, school and work activities that they really don't have a life. Socrates cautioned us centuries ago, "Beware the barrenness of a busy life." Each of us must make choices as to what is really important in our lives. I think Sidney J. Harris said it best, "The art of living consists in knowing which impulses to obey and which ones not to obey." Good advice. Logan Pearsall Smith tells us, "There are two things to aim at in life: first, to get what you want, and after that to enjoy it. Only the wisest of mankind achieve the second."

Sometimes people take themselves too seriously and their life suffers because of it. They forget life is supposed to be enjoyable. To quote Ed Foreman, "Life is for living, loving, laughing, not whining, worrying and working." We need to take life as it comes and enjoy the common everyday happenings in our life. It's the little things we need to enjoy as the really big things don't occur that often. Robert Louis Stevenson wrote, "The best things in life are nearest: breath in your nostrils, light in your eyes, flowers at your feet, duties at your hand, the path of right just before you. Then do not grasp at the stars, but do life's plain, common work as it comes, certain that daily duties and daily bread are the sweetest things in life."

Leave some time for spontaneous meaningful activities. Have some new adventures. Do some things you haven't done before. Perhaps, we need to be like President H.W. Bush, who parachuted out of a plane at an advanced age. Add something of beauty to your environment. Plant some trees whose fruit you may never see. Appreciate the wonders of life and learn to see beauty in common things. Savor small pleasures and achievements. Live your life with passion.

Think new thoughts and create new beliefs. As Gerry Spence said, "I would rather have a mind opened by wonder than one closed by belief." It's up to us to make our lives exciting and purposeful. No one can do it for us, not our spouse, not our children and not society. Life is a do-it-yourself project. Dr. William C. Menninger summed it up well when he wrote, "The amount of satisfaction you get from life depends largely on your own ingenuity, self-sufficiency, and resourcefulness. People who wait around for life to supply their satisfaction usually find boredom instead."

We need to keep busy with work or some project so we don't get bored. Boredom fosters fatigue and sucks the life out of us. Dale Carnegie had the prescription for boredom: "Are you bored with life? Then throw yourself into some work you believe in with all your heart, live it, die for it and you will find happiness that you had thought could never be yours." Change in routine is what makes the journey through life exciting. The less routine your life is, the better your life will be. It's good to take two or three days of sabbatical every now and then to alter your routine. Strive to embrace adventure, travel and new experiences. Change is what keeps the journey through life exciting. Learn to experience enchantment, fascination, playfulness, sensuality and curiosity. Live in a state of joyful expectancy. Anticipation is half the fun of life. Get out of the rut. A rut is nothing more than a grave with the ends kicked out.

Besides the people we work with on a daily basis, we need to spend time with relatives and friends to cultivate and develop relationships as people need people to really enjoy life. Relatives tend to gather together during holidays and special occasions. Friends tend to get together more frequently. Both family and friends are to be enjoyed and treasured. Marcus Tullius Cicero said, "Friendship improves happiness and abates misery, by the doubling of our joy and the dividing of our grief." Mencius put it this way, "Friends are the siblings God never gave us." Friends allow us to be ourselves. They know everything about us but accept us just the same. Most people have several acquaintances but very few true friends. If you have one or two true friends, you are very privileged. I love Leo Buscaglia's observation, "A single rose can be my garden; a single friend, my world." We need friends in various age groups – older friends to help us grow old gracefully and younger ones to help keep us young. Consider what Eleanor Roosevelt had to say about friends, "Many people will walk in and out of your life but only true friends will leave footprints in your heart." Cherish your friends as they may be your greatest possessions.

A major decision we all have to make if we live long enough is whether or not we should retire. Most people retire at age 65 or even earlier but tend to age quickly due to feelings of uselessness and boredom. The old adage that "If you don't use it, you'll lose it" is true. Entropy sets in and a downward spiral occurs. Here is what Eric Butterworth had to say about retirement, "Retirement is for going backwards, and life is only lived forward." George Burns was still working at age 99. He said, "Retirement at 65 is ridiculous. When I was 65, I still had pimples!"

Personally, I feel that retirement is an idea whose time has come and gone. We must not let ourselves get into the "retirement mentality." You can't live a life of meaning and purpose on the golf course. Most retirees sit around and waste their life. Many great people have done their best work from ages 65-95. We should be happy and grateful to be able to keep on working, as work keeps you around people and this helps to increase longevity. Work is therapy and provides a sense of accomplishment and increases our self-worth.

We need to grow old gracefully. As we get older we either get better or bitter. As the years progress and we get older, it is vitally important we maintain enthusiasm and curiosity. We are never too old to learn and we need to try new things frequently. Our goal should be "Not so much to live long as to live well," as Benjamin Franklin said. Abraham Lincoln put it this way, "It's not the years in your life that count; it's the life in your years." As we age, we should maintain an attitude of hope and expectancy. Orison Swett Marden wrote, "There is no medicine like hope, no incentive so great, and no tonic so powerful as expectation of something tomorrow."

Mark Twain stated that, "Age is an issue of mind over matter. If you don't mind, it doesn't matter." We need to be enthused about the rest of our lives. Lord Byron said, "It is very certain that the desire of life prolongs it." We can't help getting older, but we don't have to get "old." Never think of yourself as being "old." If we must retire, perhaps because of health issues, it is important that one stays busy with hobbies or other activities. Volunteer work helps to keep people feeling useful and relevant. It has been said "Life is like a game of tennis; he who serves best wins."

In order to live a happy life, we need to develop and maintain a good attitude. How you see the world matters so take charge of your attitude. Avoid negative thinking; embrace the positive. Get thicker skin so your ego doesn't get bruised so easily. Learn to accept people and the things they do without judgment. Practice forgiveness. Rise above pettiness, prejudice, judgment and resentment. Don't complain and don't tell everyone about all your troubles. Avoid the "mad, sad, shout, pout" disease. Get yourself out of the way, as life is not all about you. Feel that life is worth living and the universe is a safe place. Know that God runs the world. Withdraw only positive thoughts from your memory bank. Consider the advice from Jim Rohn, "Let others lead small lives, but not you. Let others argue over small things, but not you. Let others cry over small hurts, but not you. Let others leave their future in someone else's hands, but not you."

When your life nears its end and you pause to reflect upon your life, it's hoped you will be satisfied that you did your best. You know you will leave with few regrets and a grateful heart. Undoubtedly you have influenced countless lives in ways you cannot imagine. Ralph Waldo Emerson summed up a great life as follows: "To laugh often and much; to win the respect of intelligent people and the affection of children; to earn the appreciation of honest critics and endure the betrayal of false friends; to appreciate beauty; to find the best in others; to leave the world a little bit better whether by a healthy child, a garden patch or a redeemed social condition; to know that even one life has breathed easier because you lived. This is to have succeeded."

You attracted life to you by your thoughts and actions. Florence Scovel Shinn said, "The game of life is a game of boomerangs. Our thoughts, deeds and words return to us sooner or later with astounding accuracy." Pericles, the famous Greek statesman, orator and general of Athens, said, "What you leave behind is not what is engraved in stone monuments, but what is woven into the lives of others." Dr. Seuss said, "Don't cry because it's over, smile because it happened." An unknown author wrote, "In the end…We only regret the chances we didn't take, the relationships we were afraid to have, and the decisions we waited too long to make."

> "Nine requisites for contented living:
> Health enough to make work a pleasure.
> Wealth enough to support your needs
> Strength to battle with difficulties and overcome them.
> Grace enough to confess your sins and forsake them
> Patience enough to toll until some good is accomplished.
> Charity enough to see some good in your neighbor.
> Love enough to move you to be useful and helpful to others.
> Faith enough to make real the things of God.
> Hope enough to remove all anxious fears concerning the future."
> -Johann Wolfgang Von Goethe

DESIDERATA

Go placidly amid the noise and haste, and remember what peace there may be in silence. As far as possible without surrender, be on good terms with all persons. Speak your truth quietly and clearly; and listen to others, even the dull and ignorant; they too have their story. Avoid loud and aggressive persons, they are vexations to the spirit. If you compare yourself with others, you may become vain and bitter; for always there will be greater and lesser persons than yourself. Enjoy your achievements as well as your plans. Keep interested in your own career, however humble; it is a real possession in the changing fortunes of time. Exercise caution in your business affairs; for the world is full of trickery. But let this not blind you to what virtue there is; many persons strive for high ideals; and everywhere life is full of heroism. Be yourself. Especially, do not feign affection. Neither be cynical about love; for in the face of all aridity and disenchantment it is perennial as the grass. Take kindly the counsel of the years, gracefully surrendering the things of youth. Nurture strength of spirit to shield you in sudden misfortune. But do not distress yourself with imaginings. Many fears are born of fatigue and loneliness. Beyond a wholesome discipline, be gentle with yourself. You are a child of the universe, no less than the trees and the stars; you have a right to be here. And whether or not it is clear to you, no doubt the universe is unfolding as it should. Therefore, be at peace with God, whatever you conceive Him to be, and whatever your labors and aspirations, in the noisy confusion of life keep peace with your soul. With all its sham, drudgery and broken dreams, it is still a beautiful world. Be careful. Strive to be happy.

It's often repeated, and it never grows old.
It was found in Old Saint Paul's Church, Baltimore: dated 1692

"Yesterday is but a dream, tomorrow is only a vision.
But today well lived makes every yesterday a dream of happiness, and every tomorrow a vision of hope."
-Kalidasa

"Life is not measured by the number of breaths we take, but by the moments that take our breath away."
-Anonymous

"To live is the rarest thing in the world, most people just exist."
- Oscar Wilde

"Your life is God's gift to you, what you do with it is your gift to God."
-Anonymous

Dr. Myren D. Anderson

"Life itself is our richest treasure;
living nobly, our finest art."
-Cavett Robert

"The mass of men lead lives of quiet desperation.
What is called resignation is confirmed desperation."
-Henry David Thoreau

"Life is short, break the rules.
Forgive quickly, kiss slowly.
Love truly. Laugh uncontrollably
and never regret anything
that makes you smile.
Twenty years from now you will
be more disappointed by the things
you didn't do than by the ones you did.
So throw off the bowlines.
Sail away from the safe harbor.
Catch the trade winds in your sails."
EXPLORE. DREAM. DISCOVER.
- Mark Twain

TAKEAWAY: YOUR LIFE IS A GIFT FROM GOD. DEVOTE ENERGY TO MAKE IT A GREAT ONE.

The Spirit of God has made me, and the breath of the Almighty gives me life.
–Job 33:4

"I am come that they might have life, and that they might have it more abundantly."
–John 10:10

33

YOU NEED A FAITH TO LIVE BY

Years ago, I heard Wayne Dyer speak at a seminar and he made a very profound statement. He said, "We are not human beings having a spiritual experience; we are spiritual beings having a human experience." It seems to me we are here on planet earth to learn the lessons of life and to come to know God. If we truly are spiritual beings, our primary purpose in life is to learn about God and to develop our faith. Former President Calvin Coolidge was a man of few words but he made this observation, "We do not need more intellectual power, we need more spiritual power. We do not need more of the things that are seen, we need more of the things that are unseen." It's important we don't get caught up in worldly things. We live in a spiritual universe so we need to change our thinking from the world mass-mind thinking to spiritual thinking. The universe is obviously run by God and not by chance. There is a divine perfection in the universe as there is order and design in everything. God guides the planets in their orbits so precisely that scientists can predict where they will be in a thousand years. If the moon were just a few thousand miles closer or further away, life would be impossible on earth. The same goes for the sun. When man wants to build a better airplane, he studies birds, for example. In nature everything is perfect. King Solomon said, "Start with God-the first step in learning is bowing down to God; only fools thumb their nose at such wisdom and learning." As the scriptures remind us, "For My thoughts are not your thoughts, nor are your ways My ways," says the Lord. "For as the heavens are higher than the earth, so are My ways higher than your ways, and My thoughts higher than your thoughts. Isaiah 55:8-9

I believe that anyone who sincerely thinks about the magnificence of the universe with its order and grandeur must come to the conclusion that all of creation must have had a creator…God.

In the early 80s, I had the good fortune of hearing Rev. Bob Harrington, the Chaplain of Bourbon Street, speak at a seminar in Dallas. One of the things he said was, "You need a purpose to live for, a self that you can live with and a faith that you can live by." Rev. Harrington also spoke on the need to be balanced in all areas of our lives: physical, mental, spiritual, social, financial and family. At the time, I was doing pretty well in all areas of my life up to that point but it dawned on me that I had work to do in the spiritual realm. There is a saying, "Do not ask the Lord to guide your footsteps, if you are not willing to move your feet." I realized I needed to acknowledge a greater power. Buddha said, "Just as a candle cannot burn without fire, men cannot live without a spiritual life." As our faith grows, we realize how we can be guided by the word of God to make better decisions and choices. We tend to become more confident when we do things based on faith and inner urgings. You have a problem and pray about it and soon an answer will come through a hunch or strong feelings encouraging you to do something. Scripture says, "For I will give you words and a wisdom that none of your opponents will be able to withstand or contradict."
Luke 21:15

Know that God has a purpose for you. Feel that God is guiding you. It seems if you feed your faith, your doubts and fears starve to death. With faith you have hope and obstacles don't loom so large. General Dwight D. Eisenhower had this to say, "This is what I found out about religion: It gives you courage to make the decisions you must make in a crisis, and then the confidence to leave the result to a higher Power. Only by trust in God can a man carrying responsibility find repose." Abraham Lincoln said this, "I have been driven many times upon my knees by the overwhelming conviction that I had nowhere else to go. My own wisdom and that of all about me seemed insufficient for that day."

It seems after a while a person learns to turn his troubles over to God instead of trying to handle everything yourself. You also realize there has been a divine plan for your life and it is unfolding for you now. Everything seems to come at the perfect time and in the perfect way. If you keep your spiritual life strong it will give you inner strength, determination and peace that will take you over the rough parts in your life. We need to trust in the Power that created us so live in faith and expect the best. I read one time that, "We should trust yourself for what you see, trust God for things we can't see." As the scriptures remind us, "I think about the wisdom and the Power of the Almighty regularly and I no longer think about obstacles, delays, impediments, and failure. I know that thinking along this line builds up my faith and confidence and increases my strength and poise, "For God hath not given us the spirit of fear; but of power, and of love, and of a sound mind."
Timothy 1:7

Prayer is very powerful. People who pray and who are prayed for recover faster from illnesses and many a miracle has occurred because of prayer. It is important that we pray with confidence that our prayers will be answered. Our prayers help us to accept the good God has for us. We need to keep working to make whatever we want to occur but pray we must. As Saint Augustine said, "Pray as if everything depended on God, and work as if everything depended on you." Without faith there is little hope. Dr. Alexis Carrel said, "Prayer is the force as real as terrestrial gravity. As a physician, I have seen men, after all other therapy had failed, lifted out of disease and melancholy by serene effort of prayer. Only in prayer do we achieve that complete and harmonious assembly of body, mind and spirit which gives the frail human need its unshakable strength."

The church is the only institution in the world dedicated to helping mankind become better spiritually, morally and ethically. A strong spiritual life gives us the inner strength and determination to get us through the rough spots in our lives. In a sense we go to church to charge our batteries. It has been said that a church is not a museum for saints but a hospital for sinners. St. Francis of Assisi said, "I have been all things unholy. If God can work through me, He can work through anyone." Here is how Oscar Wilde phased it, "The only difference between the saint and the sinner is that every saint has a past and every sinner has a future."

It is important each individual should work to improve his spiritual life by reading Holy Scriptures, prayer, meditation and by performing acts of good. We need to pray daily thanking and praising God for what we have. We also need to ask for wisdom and for the ability to love and forgive. The practice of religion gives us principles to live by and increases our willpower and self-discipline. Mahatma Gandhi, put it this way, "Life without religion is life without principle, and life without principle is like a ship without a rudder." A wise person once said, "Read Proverbs every day to teach you how to get along with your fellow man. Read five Psalms every day to teach you how to get along with God."

THE TEN COMMANDMENTS

I am the Lord your God; you shall not have strange gods before me.
You shall not take the name of the Lord your God in vain.
Remember to keep holy the Lord's Day.
Honor your father and your mother.
You shall not kill.
You shall not commit adultery.
You shall not steal.
You shall not bear false witness against your neighbor.
You shall not covet your neighbor's wife
You shall not covet your neighbor's goods.

In happy moments:	Praise God
In quiet moments:	Worship God
In difficult moments:	Seek God
In painful moments:	Trust God
Every moment:	Thank God

"Eye has not seen, nor ear heard,
 nor have entered into the heart of man,
the things which God has prepared for those who love him."
1 Corinthians 2:9

"The one who doubts is like a wave of the sea, blown and tossed by the wind, for the doubter, being double-minded and unstable in every way, must not expect to receive anything from the Lord."
James 1:6-8

"He giveth power to the faint; and to them that have no might He increaseth strength." Isaiah 40:20

"For what shall it profit a man, if he shall gain the whole world, and lose his own soul?" Mark 8:36

"I will restore health unto thee, and I will heal thee of thy wounds, saith the Lord." Jeremiah 30:17

FOOTPRINTS

One night a man had a dream. He dreamed he was walking along the beach with the LORD. Across the sky flashed scenes from his life. For each scene, he noticed two sets of footprints in the sand; one belonging to him, and the other to the LORD.

When the last scene of his life flashed before him, he looked back at the footprints in the sand. He noticed that many times along the path of his life there was only one set of footprints. He also noticed that it happened at the very lowest and saddest times in his life.

This really bothered him and he questioned the LORD about it. "LORD, you said that once I decided to follow you, you'd walk with me all the way. But I have noticed that during the most troublesome times in my life, there is only one set of footprints. I don't understand why when I needed you most you would leave me."

The LORD replied, "My precious, precious child I love you and I would never leave you. During your times of trial and suffering, when you see only one set of footprints, it was then that I carried you."
-Author unknown

TAKEAWAY: GOD CAN GET ALONG WITHOUT US; WE CAN'T GET ALONG WITHOUT GOD.

Dr. Myren D. Anderson

"Beautiful young people are accidents of nature, but beautiful old people are works of art."
-Eleanor Roosevelt

"When an old man dies, it's like a library burning down."-Anonymous

34

GROWING OLD GRACEFULLY

Young people never think about getting old. They are preoccupied by the present as they live in the now. Theirs is a life of spontaneity and joy. They are constantly learning and taking most things in stride. They are excited about life and are enthusiastic about everything. Life is all about exploration and learning. They haven't learned to quit and never think of failure. They do not doubt their abilities and tend to have great dreams of future accomplishments. They have a lot of trust and tend to take risks. Thoughts of eventually getting old and dying never enter their minds. "Death is a distant rumor to the young," as Andy Rooney put it. The concept of time is practically non-existent and they tend to live their lives without deadlines. Emotions, fear, worry and anxiety rarely affect them. Life is delightful with few responsibilities.

By the time a person reaches middle age, most people are cautious and tend to take fewer risks. They have experienced some failures and disappointments and tend to see life more soberly and tend to become more serious. By then, some are having health issues and they realize they don't have the stamina and energy they once had. Harold Coffin put it this way: "Middle age is the awkward period when father time starts catching up with mother nature." For the first time some thought is given to their mortality as, perhaps, a parent has died by this time. Middle age is an extremely busy time. Someone once said that "life is so fast, it's like a husband trying to read Playboy magazine with his wife turning the pages." There are many demands of time both work and school related, primarily. Journalists Sidney J. Harris provided us with this insight, "Middle age is that perplexing time of life when we hear two voices calling us, one saying, 'why not?' and the other, 'why bother?'" Don Marquis said this, "Middle age is the time when a man is always thinking that in a week or two, he will feel as good as ever."

Eventually you look in the mirror and you realize that you, too, are getting old. You never thought it would come to this…at least not so soon. As Billy Graham said, "Growing old has been the greatest surprise of my life." And Cora Harvey Armstrong said, "Inside every older person is a younger person wondering what the hell happened?" Andy Rooney put it like this: "I didn't get old on purpose, it just happened. If you're lucky, it could happen to you."

Now, as you look at your present life you realize that you have stopped doing many of the things you did when you were younger. Hunting is now work, fishing is not as exciting etc. You read less, see fewer movies, tend to exercise less and recreational activities that you enjoyed previously tend to become more like work. Naps start to become all important. You don't sleep as well but your appetite is good so you tend to gain weight. Perhaps you have retired early. Now you have nothing to do and no reason to wake up every day. Depression gradually overtakes you and sucks the life out of you. Without work you become less confident. You have doubts whether your savings will last. You spend time reviewing your doctor bills looking for mistakes. You keep several doctors busy and you know you are taking too much medication. Your conversation becomes more and more about disease and aches and pains. You are not happy as life becomes drudgery as every day is the same. You didn't do anything yesterday and today is the same. A big day is when you go and see several doctors. Perhaps, you have moved out of your home you have lived in for 50 years and now you're living in an apartment in a retirement community or in a senior center. You miss your home. Everybody around you is old and they all have aches and pains and ailments they love to tell you about. Leaving your home has caused a lot of stress and all of a sudden you feel a lot older. You think to yourself, "If I had known I was going to live this long, I would have taken better care of myself."

As a chiropractor for 50-plus years, I have had the privilege of treating many elderly patients. Some were old at age 50; others were still young at age 90. What is the difference? In my view, the people who were still active, healthy and enthusiastic in old age were grateful for having reached an advanced age and they viewed getting older as a gift and a privilege not as a burden. They didn't act "old." They were still enthusiastic. Those patients who were old in years but actually were young were not old in spirit and didn't act old. They put old on hold and never allowed their chronological age to limit their potential. Henry David Thoreau wrote, "None are so old as those who have outlived enthusiasm." You don't stop being enthusiastic and excited about life because you grow old, you grow old because you stopped being enthusiastic and being excited about life. You grow old when you lose interest in living. A person who ages well doesn't live his life according to his age. In other words, they don't let their age determine how he or she feels. Satchel Paige, the great baseball pitcher, put it like this, "How old would you be, if you didn't know how old you are?"

Patients that did the best were those that continued to work, either in their profession or in a part-time job to keep themselves busy. Hobbies such as woodworking, painting, knitting and sewing were also helpful. Farmers who had sons who took over the farm also did very well, as they could be called upon for advice and to help in the field during the busy planting and harvest times. This type of activity helps to keep older people feeling useful and earning a few extra dollars helps as well.

When you live a life of purpose, you are living, not just existing. It's better to wear out than to rust out. Redirect your activities and your interests when you retire. Change is what makes the journey through life interesting and exciting. Embrace adventure, travel and new experiences. Think outside the casket! Never let an "old" person inhabit your body. Decide to be a youthful older person. Getting older is not so much a matter of age; it is more a lack of movement and how you think. Get moving and you will minimize many of the infirmities of age. I like what George Burns said about aging, "You can't help getting older, but you don't have to get old." He also said, "Retirement at 65 is ridiculous. When I was 65, I still had pimples." George Burns went on to entertain his audiences for nearly another 34 years and died at 100 years. It seems there is an art to aging gracefully. The great Casey Stengel said, "The trick is growing up without growing old." Consider the words of Francis Bacon, "I will never be an old man. To me, old age is always 15 years older than I am." What a wonderful thought! Get off your butt and do some exercises. Walking is a wonderful aerobic exercise which develops endurance and improves cardiovascular health. Walking also helps to clear your mind and gives you time to think. Having a dog is a good way to force yourself to walk. Dogs are wonderful companions and they enrich your life to an extent that is hard to describe. Your dog is always up for anything you decide to do, whether retrieving a ball or going for a walk. Dogs are the epitome of enthusiasm and some tend to rub off on the dog owner.

Those folks who age well continue to read and learn. Many learn how to use a computer. They socialize more but talk less about their ailments. Advanced age is not for the faint of heart. As Art Linkletter said, "Old age is not for sissies." Older folks who are aging well tend to be very active. They exercise and take long walks daily. Many are avid golfers, hunters or fishermen. John Adams offered this wisdom, "Old minds are like old horses: you must exercise them if you wish to keep them in working order."

Another thing I noticed about those folks who are aging well is they became more spiritual. I believe they were confident they would live on in another life and they were at peace with death. I think they understood life was not about maintaining control and you need to let go and enjoy the trip. They did not seem to be fighting getting older. They know they are not going to live forever so they just live one day at a time.

Another attribute of those who did well in advanced age is they didn't try so hard to make themselves look forever young. They accepted their gray and thinning hair, wrinkles and other signs of aging. Imagine how insecure some people are that need to have face lifts and other temporary fixes only to look even older in the end. Coco Chanel said, "Nothing makes a woman look so old as trying desperately hard to look young." I think Ralph Waldo Emerson said it best, "The age of a woman doesn't mean a thing. The best tunes are played on the oldest fiddles." "An archaeologist is the best husband a woman can have. The older she gets the more interested he is in her." -Agatha Christie

Confucius observed, "The great man is he who has not lost his child's heart." It's okay to play games and climb trees. We should retain the ability to have fun, laugh and enjoy life with pure joy. It is important that as we age, we don't dwell on what we have lost but instead dwell on what we have left. Know you're never too old to set a few more goals or to dream another dream. It's good to have a positive attitude about life. Perhaps Doug Larson said it best, "The aging process has you firmly in its grasp if you never get the urge to throw a snowball." Seniors who age well are comfortable with their age-but they don't always act their age. They tend to fill their days with fun and meaningful activities.

Another characteristic of those who age well is they tend to exercise regularly, to eat moderately and in general take better care of themselves. They are careful not to be overmedicated and are not preoccupied with disease and suffering. If they have a medical issue they tend to keep quiet about it and not talk about it incessantly. Mark Victor Hanson came up with 10 ways to add 10 years to your life:

Exercise regularly
Eat less
Get eight hours of sleep
Add humor to your life
Start your day right
Use alcohol in moderation
Refrain from smoking
Have a sense of curiosity
Have happy relationships
Have a passion for life

Another common trait of those who age well is a tendency to serve others by volunteering. Many of these folks are tireless and spend countless hours making quilts for the needy, driving older patients to doctors, helping out at senior meals, etc. It's well to remember volunteers have troubles of their own; many don't feel particularly well and some have lost their spouses. They have gone through hardships but appreciate life and understand what it means to persevere, overcome and to continue living. They realize age is not a barrier and the only limitation you have is what you put on yourself. They don't dwell on what they have lost but instead concentrate on what they have left.

Do you think you are too old to accomplish anything? Here are some folks who contributed into their 80s and beyond:
Winston Churchill wrote, A History of the English-Speaking Peoples, at age 82. Claude Pepper was still serving in congress at age 88. At 91 years of age, Armand Hammer headed Occidental Petroleum. George Burns was still entertaining at age 99. Grandma Moses was still painting at age 101. Socrates learned to play musical instruments at 80 years of age. Michelangelo was still painting and sculpting at age 88.

We should never regret growing older. It is a privilege denied to many. Growing older is the price we pay for not dying young. Think of all the folks killed at an early age or struck down in the prime of life. Yes, life is a gift; never take it for granted. Make the rest of your life the best of your life…a showcase for positive living. They say that life is like a roll of toilet paper. The closer it gets to the end, the faster it goes…so hang on and enjoy the ride. Personally, I feel that I have lived too long to die young but I feel I am a long way from being old. It's a nice place to be.

> "The goal is to live and love
> long with health and have a
> rapid decline right before
> the end."
> Andrew Weil, M.D.

As we advance in years, it is important that we don't consider ourselves senior citizens or "old." Get comfortable with your age. Don't talk about being old and don't talk to others about your aches and pains. The more you talk about your troubles the more you will have. Don't act like an "old" person would and don't cry because it's almost over; smile because it happened. Appreciate the fact that wrinkles don't hurt! I love what Rose Kennedy had to say about getting older, "I know not age, nor weariness nor defeat." If anybody had an excuse to be down-hearted it would have been her. Instead, she was upbeat until the very end. What a remarkable lady!

In the end, we must all die. But if we have lived life well, we probably will have few regrets. Leo Tolstoy had this to say, "But there is only one way to prepare for death and that is to live well." As Christians, we believe in life after death. I quote Helen Keller, "Death is no more than passing from one room into another. But there's a difference for me, you know. Because in that room I shall be able to see." Wow!

> A skeptic walks up to a Zen master and asks:
> "Is there life after death?"
> "How should I know?" the master replied.
> "But you're a Zen master!"
> "Yes," the Zen master says, "but not a dead one."
> -Zen Mondo

> "In youth the days are short
> and the years are long.
> In old age the years are short
> and the days' long."
> -Pope Paul VI

"You are as young as your faith,
as old as your doubt; as young
as your self-confidence, as old as your
fear; as young as your hope,
as old as your despair."
-Samuel Ullman

"But it is our duty…to resist old age; to compensate for its defects by watchful care; to fight against it as we would fight against disease; to practice moderate exercise; and to take just enough food and drink to restore our strength and not to overburden it. Nor, indeed, are we to give our attention solely to the body; much greater care is due to the mind and soul; for they; too, like lamps, grow dim with time, unless we keep them supplied with oil…intellectual activity gives buoyancy to the mind."
-Cicero

"The hour of departure has arrived and we go our way. I to die, and you to live. Which is better? Only God knows."
-Socrates

TAKEAWAY: GETTING OLDER IS INEVITABLE;
FEELING AND ACTING OLD IS OPTIONAL.

Dr. Myren D. Anderson

Become The Person You Were Meant To Be

ABOUT THE AUTHOR

DR. MYREN D. ANDERSON

Dr. Myren D. Anderson is currently in his fifty-sixth year of Chiropractic practice. He has attended hundreds of seminars, conventions and conferences where he learned valuable lessons from world-class speakers and leaders from Art Linkletter to Zig Ziglar. Dr. Anderson is an enthusiastic, outdoors man who enjoys hunting, fishing and adventure, in general. He also enjoys travel to interesting places and is an avid reader and has an extensive personal library.

Dr. Anderson and his wife, Elaine, have been married for fifty-eight years. They have five sons and a daughter, nine grandchildren and a great granddaughter. They make their home in the greatest small town in the country, Stephen, Minnesota.

BECOME THE PERSON YOU WERE MEANT TO BE is his first book.

Made in the USA
Monee, IL
25 February 2024

53519838R00125